HOMESCHOOLERS' SUCCESS STORIES

15 Adults and 12 Young People Share the Impact That Homeschooling Has Made on Their Lives

LINDA DOBSON

PRIMA PUBLISHING
3000 Lava Ridge Court
Roseville, CA 95661
1-800-632-8676
www.primalifestyles.com

Photograph of Amy Burritt by Genesis Photographic; David Beihl and Alex Trebek by Maria Stenzel © 1999 National Geographic Society; Rikki Scandora © 1998 Stephanie Felix; Melissa Sconyers by Rand Alhadeff; Gaylen Kaup by Meg Pukel

PRIMA PUBLISHING and colophon are trademarks of Prima Communications Inc., registered with the United States Patent and Trademark Office.

Library of Congress Cataloging-in-Publication Data

Dobson, Linda
    Homeschoolers' success stories : 15 adults and 12 young people share the impact that homeschooling has made on their lives/Linda Dobson.
        p.   cm. — (Prima's home learning library)
    ISBN 0-7615-2255-7
    1. Home schooling—United States—Case studies. I. Title. II. Series.

LC40 .D64 2000
371.04'2—dc21   00-032693
                                                                                            CIP

00 01 02 03 HH 10 9 8 7 6 5 4 3 2 1
Printed in the United States of America

How to Order

Single copies may be ordered from Prima Publishing, 3000 Lava Ridge Court, Roseville, CA 95661; telephone (800) 632-8676, EXT. 4444. Quantity discounts are also available. On your letterhead, include information concerning the intended use of the books and the number of books you wish to purchase.

Visit us online at www.primalifestyles.com

To Charles and Evelyn Winkelried,
who didn't say anything even though they thought I was nuts to
homeschool and who now have a grandson featured in this book

Contents

FOREWORD

by Reed Colfax

Virtually all parents seek the best possible education for their children.

For many parents, however, the education they perceive as the best is simply not available. Many factors, including financial resources and geographic location, limit the forms of education parents can offer their children. Some types of education are not even considered because their availability or potential benefits are unknown. Homeschooling is a prime example of such a form of education. For years, most parents have been unaware of homeschooling as an educational option. Recently, however, with the numbers of homeschoolers increasing, homeschooling has begun to enter the national consciousness as a realistic means to educate children. Today there is a good probability that a colleague, friend, or relative is homeschooling or has been homeschooled. Of course, despite the presence of homeschoolers in all segments of society, many parents remain skeptical of the efficacy of homeschooling. Such skepticism, however, becomes increasingly difficult to maintain as more and more stories of successful homeschooling experiences continue to unfold.

When my parents began homeschooling in the early 1970s, they knew no stories of homeschoolers, successful or otherwise. At the time, homeschooling was not a viable schooling choice being considered by parents throughout the country. Homeschooling was more of an emergency stop-gap for those parents who had no other options. Our family was not aware of anyone else homeschooling when we chose not to attend the local elementary school. Homeschooling presented itself as the only possible means for me and my brothers to begin our educations. The only traditional schooling available was the local public school, which was a 20-minute drive away when the unmaintained dirt roads were passable. Our family had just purchased an isolated piece of undeveloped property with no roads, no structures, or any other amenities. The kids were critical to carving out a place to live. If we had been in school for 6 or 7 hours a day, we would not have been available to burn brush or level land. Homeschooling was a necessity, but it was only temporary. Once our land was nominally developed and the roads were better maintained, we were given the standing offer to attend the public school whenever we should choose. But homeschooling was working, and it did not appear that we were missing any great educational opportunities at the local school. As the years passed, the temporary solution evolved into a permanent program.

Today homeschooling is frequently chosen, at the outset of a child's schooling, as a long-term way to educate the child. This choice is made now even where other educational options are present. As parents make such a choice, they can take comfort in homeschooling books, homeschooling support groups, homeschooling conferences, and homeschooling curricula. But the largest numbers of parents will be persuaded that homeschooling is a legitimate educational option by the stories of those who have been homeschooled. The tales of the homeschooled will answer the questions and allay the fears that all parents have as they consider starting to homeschool. They will also allow many unfamiliar with homeschooling to see its potential value.

For most, it takes the presence of a real, live homeschooler to destroy the many deep-seated preconceptions about homeschooling. Those who believe that homeschoolers cannot possibly be fully socialized or that homeschooling cannot possibly provide a well-rounded education will likely hold those beliefs until they see evidence of "normal" and "educated" homeschoolers. The stories of homeschoolers, therefore, become very important to demonstrating the viability of homeschooling.

Homeschooling will fare well if it must rely upon its students and graduates to advertise its virtues. My first exposure to a substantial number of other homeschoolers came many years after I was finished homeschooling when I attended a homeschooling conference. I marveled at the homeschoolers. Any parent would have been proud to have had any one of them as a child. Most memorable was a panel of homeschooling teens who talked about their experiences in homeschooling. The teens were articulate and mature, and they demonstrated a confidence that is absent from most their age. I could see the fear and apprehension evaporating from the parents in the audience who were considering homeschooling their own children. By simply being themselves, these teens were the most effective possible advertisement for homeschooling. It was impossible to watch these kids without considering what our youth would be like if they were all homeschooled.

The stories of homeschoolers certainly ease the decision of whether to homeschool. The stories also contain valuable lessons for those who are homeschooling. Every homeschooler can recite good and bad aspects of their experiences. Mistakes have been and will continue to be made by homeschoolers. Knowing the stories of those who came before will, however, allow parents and children to avoid a number of pitfalls. In my family, the younger siblings watched as Grant, the oldest child in the family, blazed trails for his education. At times the paths he chose led to dead-end, non-productive places. When they did, the younger brothers would choose other paths. We all thank Grant for the time he spent laboring through a "new math." He did not learn a single new useful math skill, but the rest of us thought it was time well-wasted.

At the same time, we did not always choose to follow Grant's successful endeavors. Homeschooling allowed such freedom and flexibility that even where we saw one brother have a good experience, we were not compelled to follow. Unlike traditional schools, where teachers and administrators often attempt to recreate precisely the system that was successful for some students, homeschooling allows children to discover their own ways to successful educations. In our family, my two older brothers learned to write effectively at a young age. Grant had written a book before he was in his teens, and Drew's extensive diary entries chronicled every moment of our family's experience. I, on the other hand, wrote nothing. With no pressure to write a book or chronicle a life, I waited until my late teens when a way to learn to write presented itself. At fifteen, I began editing and writing for the local running club newsletter, and ever since, writing has been my favorite aspect of schooling and work. Every homeschooler will have similar stories of right and wrong turns that can provide guides and ideas for subsequent homeschoolers.

For parents seeking the best education for their children, stories of homeschoolers are invaluable. Such stories will make parents aware of the possibilities with homeschooling and demonstrate how homeschooling can work. *Homeschoolers' Success Stories* presents an unparalleled set of homeschooling stories. If these profiles had been available when my parents began homeschooling, it would have greatly eased our road through homeschooling.

These profiles do not proselytize but simply provide a glimpse into a world unknown to many. The homeschoolers profiled tell their stories and in so doing demonstrate in no uncertain terms that homeschooling stands as a truly viable option for educating our children.

REED COLFAX and his three brothers were homeschooled in Northern California. The experiences of the Colfax family are chronicled in two books authored by Reed's parents, David and Micki Colfax: *Hard Times in Paradise* and *Homeschooling for Excellence*.

Reed, along with two of his brothers, graduated from Harvard; he then attended Yale Law School. After graduating, Reed served as a judicial law clerk to United States District Court Judge Thelton Henderson, and then completed a two-year fellowship with the NAACP Legal Defense and Educational Fund, Inc., litigating racial discrimination cases. Reed currently serves as a staff attorney for the Fair Housing Project of the Washington Lawyers' Committee for Civil Rights and Urban Affairs. In that position, Reed litigates cases on behalf of victims of housing discrimination in the Washington, D.C., metropolitan area.

INTRODUCTION

An introduction is a wonderful place for a writer to reveal to her readers where she is coming from before they grab a cup of tea and snuggle down with her book (at least that's how I hope folks read my books). Some of what the people featured in this book have to say about education may make you uncomfortable; it's better you know it right from the start rather than discover it halfway through the book. If you don't want to hear any more, put the book back on the shelf and don't buy it. I have no desire to deliver to you anything you don't want to hear. I'm sure it has something to do with knowing humans' predisposition to kill the messenger.

But I'm counting on the fact that you, like many parents, know that something frightening is happening to our youth. Record numbers of children are being labeled learning disordered or placed on behavior altering medications like Ritalin. They are turning to illegal drugs and alcohol at younger and younger ages. Cliques, bullying, and generalized torment determine a child's standing in the school-centered pecking order, readying these future taxpayers for class distinctions in adult life. Hopelessness permeates the lives of many, who then turn to violence, including unprecedented mass murders committed, as a rule, at the very schools they are by compulsory attendance laws (with few exceptions) forced to attend. If any of these trends bothers you, you just may want to continue reading.

Sure, there's more than enough blame to throw around, and it gets thoroughly scattered. We've blamed parents, teachers, school administrators, doctors, politicians, police, lawyers, and clergy. We've blamed lack of money, too much money, television, games, music, computers, and movies. We've blamed Wall Street, Main Street, Washington, D.C., Hollywood, and every state capitol in between. So who and what are really to blame?

Maybe it's time for us to consider the notion that blaming any or all of the above who, what, and wheres isn't helping. Blame has been thrown everywhere—what a clue! I think this tells us that whatever the culprit is, it's pervasive in our culture, and steadily eating at it, like a spreading cancer. Every one, every thing, every where can be blamed for contributing something to the problem.

Maybe it's time for us to consider the notion that the cultural cancer is affecting our children, and that rather than address the cancer's symptoms (all of the above), it's time to look for the tumor and cut it out.

In this book, you will read about lives in which at least some of the "compulsory school age" years were spent outside of school. Has freedom, however brief, from the institutional lifestyle of schools made a difference? I think the people you will meet in these pages show that this freedom does make a difference. As you meet these people and discover what they have to say about life and learning now that they are on the far side of homeschooling, you can decide for yourself.

I've been aware of some of the people in this book for a long time. As the writer of the homeschooling news column for *Home Education Magazine*, I'd gotten word of their achievements through the media, but always in stories that left me wanting to know more about them. Which of the countless homeschooling approaches did they experience? Did they enjoy homeschooling? What were their thoughts on homeschooling's role in what they'd accomplished? Could what they discovered about learning while homeschooling help concerned parents see their own children's learning in a clearer light?

Even with all the wonderful stories I was aware of, I put out the word to the homeschooling community, via email and print announcements, that I was looking for more. After all, I had a publisher willing to produce a work on homeschooling that, instead of adding to the astonishing number of how-to-homeschool books, could help concerned parents see why-to-homeschool through the eyes of adults who experienced it. While we were at it, I decided to include a glimpse into the lives of some currently homeschooling children, as well.

Homeschooling is the world's most flexible approach to education. Being so, different families bend and shape it to meet their children's needs. This means that no two families go about it in quite the same manner. I wanted the largest selection of stories possible to choose from so that readers could see that homeschooling succeeds in a vast array of manifestations.

The array of possibilities presented to me with the wonderful support of the homeschooling community did not disappoint. You will meet folks who homeschooled for a very brief time, most of their school years, or moved back and forth between school and home. Their families chose homeschooling for reasons religious, philosophical, and utilitarian. Some focused on academic achievement, and others gave just enough time to academics so they could spend more time pursuing individual interests. Some traveled and others remained in small towns, big cities, or the suburbs. They approached homeschooling alone, with the aid of correspondence courses, with purchased curriculum, or with tutors.

Adults who were homeschooled for all or part of their early years are increasingly among us—as neighbors, friends, relatives, co-workers, employers, church mates. What have they learned from their experience, and does what they learned impact their lives today? Does learning without school, removing the influence of compulsory attendance, affect family life, chosen work, or even the way one goes about learning through adulthood? If so, are there any implications for our culture as an increasing number of citizens reach adulthood with similar "years spent outside of school"? (Please keep in mind that an increasing number of folks have also spent all of their compulsory school-age years outside of school.)

After 15 years as a homeschooling parent, after receiving mail and phone calls from countless homeschoolers for almost as long, after visiting face to face with countless other homeschooling parents at conferences across the country, and after collecting and reading media reports on homeschooling for almost 8 years in my capacity as news editor and columnist for *Home Education Magazine,* I am convinced that the implications for our society of childhood spent outside of school are positive ones.

While working on *Homeschooling the Early Years: Your Complete Guide to Successfully Homeschooling the 3- to 8-Year-Old Child,* I surveyed experienced homeschoolers about what they saw as the practice's greatest benefits. Their top five answers bear repeating, as the benefits they witnessed on a personal level are the same ones that will benefit our society as a whole.

Homeschooling parents witness, and society benefits from:

- Improved academic abilities—homeschoolers learn how to learn
- Expanded social opportunities—homeschoolers participate in social activity with the general population of all ages
- Stronger family bonds—homeschoolers build sturdy families, the foundational building blocks of a healthy society
- Safer surroundings—homeschoolers learn in an atmosphere free of violence, drugs, bullying, sexual harassment, or threats thereof
- Improved physical, mental, and emotional health—(anecdotally at least) homeschoolers enjoy relatively wholesome lifestyles

I am convinced that compulsory school attendance is the cultural cancer producing such frightening effects in our children.

Homeschooling families, among others turning to alternatives to government school attendance, are voting with their feet for a cure to the dis-ease their children experience. My sincerest hope is that the following stories will show you that cure in action. It's a simple one, really, and only you as a parent can administer it outside the institution. I share these stories so that your children, too, may recover or, better yet, never be exposed at all.

I

The Homeschooling Legacy

Once upon a time, a caveman pointed at a plant and grunted for his son to take a look—the world's first homeschooler. To date there are no records of a troglodyte who thought it would be a good idea to gather all the little troglodytes together in one cave, far away from field and forest, to review stick drawings of those plants that, if eaten, could kill you.

The Many Approaches to Homeschooling

Are you wondering if our caveman was really homeschooling? Join the crowd! Homeschooling is the world's most flexible educational approach. As such, its practice looks different from household to household, and it sounds different from description to description. Some would say of the caveman, "Yes, he's homeschooling"; others would say, "There are no books or lectures or desks involved so, no, he is not."

A nice reward of homeschooling is that because you take the responsibility for it, because you are the one shaping, modifying, and experimenting with it until it best serves your child's educational needs, you get to define it for your own family—as did the families you will meet in this book. Even so, you will see that they all have something in common, an idea I hope you will keep in the back of your mind as you read their stories. No matter whether one observer would call what they did homeschooling and another would not, *these adults and children all spent some period of childhood growing in freedom, liberated from compulsory school attendance.*

Families have always turned to homeschooling for many different reasons, from the practical to the philosophical. With these myriad starting points, those who begin with the notion of "homeschooling" soon set off on diverse and divergent paths.

To illustrate this, let's use the analogy of climbing a mountain to describe the process of homeschooling. Hundreds of thousands of families set out to reach the summit of the same mountain. Some start by packing up everything they own. Others choose to travel lightly. Various families walk, drive, fly, or take a train to get to the foot of the mountain.

Arriving at the mountain's base, families choose various sides from which to begin their climb: north, south, east, west, and all points in between. Some move slowly, others quickly. Some set their sights only on the mountain peak, others tend to emphasize the hike. Some employ a guide, others follow previously traveled trails, still others blaze their own paths. After a given period of time, and even though they're all headed for the same mountain peak, each family: (a) has experienced a unique journey; and (b) stands at a location unlike the others.

Now, imagine that at one moment in time we ask all the families to describe the view before them. Those who have climbed at the most leisurely pace aren't high enough to see the lakes dotting the landscape below that the quicker hikers report. Those who have their sights set on the mountain peak can see even higher peaks from their vantage point. Those emphasizing the journey provide detailed reports on the flora and fauna spotted along the way. Those who began from the north side report different flora and fauna from those who began from the south.

Each family—indeed, each individual within each family—views the journey up the mountain from a different perspective. All are headed for the same peak; all are homeschooling. Yet the "views" are different for each.

Choices

All these different paths mean that homeschooling parents can choose from an array of "curricula-in-a-box" (traditional schooling at home), rely on curricula for some subjects and not others (relaxed or eclectic homeschooling), or follow their children's interests in lieu of a curriculum (interest-led or unschooling).

And the choices continue. Today, many states accommodate parents who want their child to take some classes at school and some at home. Depending on their viewpoint, parents term this approach to learning as supplementing government schooling with homeschooling or supplementing homeschooling with government schooling. Some homeschooling support groups grow large enough to offer their own classes, taught by volunteer parents or by hired teachers.

Homeschooling charter schools have become increasingly popular. Many states license these apparently alternative schools, founded or operated by parents, teachers, or businesses. The schools receive a "charter" from an existing government school system, then operate free from *some* of the regulations placed on the mainstream school. Government funds enter the equation, for when homeschooled children spend X amount of time at a desk in a school, that school receives a financial benefit. Some homeschooling parents worry about the accountability, reporting, assessments, and control tied to the funds, all means that quietly but ultimately erode family autonomy. He who pays the bills gets to make the major decisions.

Still other parents are beginning to recognize the wisdom of "half a loaf of bread is better than none," choosing to provide their children a bit of homeschooling after school, on weekends, or during school breaks and vacations. Homeschooling, with the many options available today, has certainly come a long way since the modern movement's humble beginnings.

A Brief History of American Homeschooling

Many regard homeschooling as a new educational phenomenon, but that is simply a reflection of the bias of our times. If somehow we could help our caveman see into the future, he would regard government-sponsored schools as the variant, as would the majority of his descendants at least until the middle of the nineteenth century. Until then, the mostly agrarian American society lived a family-centered lifestyle; education happened at home, if only by default.

> **Still other parents are choosing to provide their children a bit of home-schooling after school, on weekends, or during school breaks and vacations.**

Through involvement in daily life's work, children gathered knowledge of everything from growing food, construction, caring for livestock, and making tools, clothing, soap, and whatever few other resources they *needed.* Lessons necessary to turn them into readers, writers, and cipherers proficient enough to handle their own affairs and grow into responsible citizens took only a fraction of the time that they consume today, and they stopped when the season demanded their time and attention in the field or elsewhere. The lessons were provided by parents, older siblings, or perhaps a young single woman hired for a pittance by the community's families to teach the basics. No laws existed, though, to compel (force) attendance.

The development of the modern educational system may be said to have been well on its way (over the objections of many teachers, parents, and public press) with the first state compulsory attendance law, courtesy of Massachusetts in 1852, coupled with the shift from an agrarian to an industrial society and its accompanying, vigorously enforced child labor laws. Modern-day switches from one pedagogical plan to another are hard enough to keep up with, but the complete story of how we got to our current state of school affairs takes so many twists and convolutions that I can only recommend that you read John Taylor Gatto's *The Underground History of American Education: A Schoolteacher's Intimate Investigation into the Problem of Modern Schooling* (The Oxford Village Press, 2000) to attempt a complete understanding of the evolution.

It's only because we are now looking back over a 150-year history of government-supported, compulsorily attended schooling, one that most of us accepted as perfectly natural as we grew up (as did our parents and many of our grandparents), that homeschooling is perceived as something new. The current homeschooling movement is only new in that it has occurred following compulsory attendance laws and has grown sizeable enough to be noticed.

It is difficult to peg the exact origin of modern homeschooling. Some might say the seeds were being planted in the sixties and seventies by educational reformers and authors who questioned both schooling's methods and results. Notable among them are Ivan Illich (*Deschooling Society,* Harper & Row, 1971), Charles E. Silberman (*Crisis in the Classroom: The Remaking of American Education,* Random House, 1970), and the prolific John Holt (*How Children Fail,* Dell Publishing, 1964; *How Children Learn,* Dell Publishing, 1967; *What Do I Do Monday?* Dell Publishing, 1970), a teacher who eventually gave up his original vision of school reform as hopeless. He began advocating instead no school for youngsters, and in 1977 began publishing *Growing Without Schooling,* a magazine that continues today even though John passed away in 1985.

Around the same time, Dr. Raymond and Dorothy Moore were busy conducting and collecting early childhood education research. They, too, began publishing articles and books that questioned the wisdom of conventional schooling with a focus on the harm that can be created by rushing children prematurely into the existing school regimen (see *Better Late Than Early: A New Approach to Your Child's Education,* Reader's Digest Press, 1975; *School Can Wait,* Hewitt Research Foundation, 1985).

By the late seventies and early eighties, the message was spreading. The nationally acclaimed *Home Education Magazine* made its humble start in 1983. As the number of homeschoolers slowly grew so did the number of support groups focused on helping other parents get started in homeschooling. Networking homeschoolers worked to educate legislators and eventually changed state laws that prohibited the practice. The grassroots movement kept growing.

In the 1980s, changes in the tax regulations for Christian schools forced the smaller among them to close down by the hundreds. Suddenly, the parents of the students attending these schools were faced with a choice between government school attendance and homeschooling. For many, this really wasn't a choice at all, and these Christian families became part of a large second wave of homeschooling, joining earlier homeschoolers and boosting the numbers to record highs. Christian curriculum providers, already well-established businesses that had just lost a large chunk of their original market, followed the money and easily courted the new market of homeschooling parents.

Since then, the media has identified yet another wave of homeschoolers—"the mainstreamers." These are families from every conceivable religious, economic, political, and philosophical background in the United States. This wave has been impelled by: homeschooling's greater visibility as an educational option; local, state, and national homeschooling support groups; easy networking and information sharing via the Internet and e-mail; and continuing government-school problems, such as dumbed-down curriculum, violence, drugs, bullying, and more. These forces have brought up the number of home-schooled children in the United States an estimated 15 to 20% each year for the last 15 years. The ballpark figure now stands at two million and growing.

Homeschoolers Past and Present

Numbers are only part of any historical retelling. More interesting are the lives of the people who made that history. And what better way to review America's history of homeschooling, in a book about success stories, than with homeschoolers' success stories from the past to the present? Homeschooling parents Mac and Nancy Plent felt the same way. While researching their book, *An A in Life: Famous Homeschoolers,* they "began to joke that it looked like almost everybody we want our kids to learn about didn't go to school," recalls Nancy.

The couple's work began as a response to Mac's frustration with the disapproval they encountered when telling people they home-schooled their children; this was in the late 1970s and early 1980s when most people didn't know what homeschooling was. Mac reasoned that if "he could just name a couple of well-known people who were homeschooled, he might be able to silence the critics," writes Nancy in the introduction to their book. "He found he could flip through the *Dictionary of American Biographies,* the encyclopedia, or any reference work that included biographical entries, and stories of home education jumped out at him."

> **Christian families became part of a large second wave of home-schooling, joining earlier homeschoolers and boosting the numbers to record highs.**

The Plents have kindly let me borrow from their much more extensive body of work for this tour of history. On the tour, we visit the lives of some folks who, again, whether one person would call what they did homeschooling and another would not, grew in freedom from compulsory school attendance. The accounts of well-known people from the past will provide a framework for comparison to the modern stories coming up, especially if you pay particular attention to the activities that filled the time freed from school attendance.

Homeschooled Presidents

"With little early schooling, he accompanied his father to France at the age of 11, already keeping a journal which developed into one of the most famous of diaries," says the *Dictionary of American Biographies* about John Adams, the second president of the United States, who served from 1797 to 1801.

President from 1861 to 1865, Abraham Lincoln "had a few short weeks of schooling under Andrew Crawford. Two years later he attended a school . . . for a few more weeks. After an internship for a year, he picked up a few instructions. These schools were called blab schools . . . all of the students recited aloud together and the master measured their diligence by the volume of the babel. These short intervals marked the end of Lincoln's formal education," relates Benjamin Thomas in *Abraham Lincoln* (Knopf, 1952).

Reaching into the twentieth century, we find Woodrow Wilson who, as a boy, "had no systematic early education . . . (but had) contact with cultivated minds and the constant instruction of parents who were devotedly interested in his progress," explains Ray Stainnard Baker in *Woodrow Wilson: Life and Letters. Youth, 1856–1890* (Doubleday, 1927). A young man who didn't read until he was 11 years old, in part because so many people would read aloud to him the many books in his home, Wilson "impressed people with his individuality," Baker continues. "They said he was distinctive, different. Later, writers trying to unlock the mystery, used such expressions as 'baffling, complex, prophetic' . . . He began early to 'command his own development.'"

The United States has had 43 presidents. A little more than one-third of them, or 17, received the type of education that today we call homeschooling.

A Few Other Homeschooled Presidents

Grover Cleveland

James Garfield

Andrew Jackson

Thomas Jefferson

Franklin Delano Roosevelt

Theodore Roosevelt

George Washington

Homeschooled Business People and Entrepreneurs

Publishing industry history is dotted with homeschoolers. At 15, *New York Tribune* founder Horace Greeley (1811–1872) wasn't in school but apprenticing in a Vermont newspaper office. Perhaps you don't recognize the name Adolph Ochs, but you know the newspaper he started: the *New York Times.* At the age of 11, Adolph (1858–1935) was an office boy at the *Knoxville Chronicle.* Although he did receive a bit of local schooling, the *Dictionary of American Biographies* reports that his "parents were good substitutes for a more formal education" and that he considered the printing office his "high school and university."

Then there's Dr. Orison Swett Marden, born in 1850. His mother died when he was 3, his father when he was 7. "His guardian wasted no time in sending him off as a hired boy,"

At 15, *New York Tribune* founder Horace Greeley wasn't in school but apprenticing in a Vermont newspaper office.

reports a 1997 editorial in *Success* magazine. For 10 years, Orison was "regularly whipped, beaten, kicked, cuffed and nearly starved . . . By his teens, he had lived entirely in the backwoods."

Fate placed in Marden's path an 1859 book titled *Self Help,* by Samuel Smiles, a Scot. The book's true stories about perseverant, energetic, and hard-working boys inspired Marden to vow to "climb out of poverty and become the American Samuel Smiles." He "wangled his way" into New Hampshire's Colby Academy and was a wealthy young man by the time he was 32. In 1900, he fulfilled his promise to become the American Samuel Smiles with the first issue of his publication, *Success.*

Many homeschooling families immediately recognize the bright colors and interesting content of Dorling Kindersley (DK) books, CD-ROMs, videos, and atlases. DK's founder and chairman, Peter Kindersley, was homeschooled as a child and worked as a book illustrator before hitting the big time as a publisher. His company Web site (www.dklearning.co.uk) boasts a quote from Peter: "The home is the first school, and parents are the first teachers." He also encourages home business opportunities for DK sales associates.

The business world also has its share of homeschoolers. Bank of America's founder, Amadeo Giannini (1870–1947), "would have an early supper after school, then bed until nearly midnight [when] the best part of his life would begin again as he followed his stepfather around . . . asking questions about his business. The boy followed his father around the docks from midnight to seven in the morning . . . At his mother's insistence, he took a few months' course in business college, then at 15 decided the schoolroom had given him all he wanted out of it" (Julian Dana, *A. P. Giannini: Giant of the West,* Prentice, 1947).

Every day millions of Americans patronize the businesses of not one but three young men who chose an early end to compulsory school attendance and who thought feeding Americans—quickly— might be a good business idea.

Colonel Harland Sanders (1890–1980), whose cartoon image is permanently etched in the minds of television viewers as the white-haired "Duke of Drumsticks" and who started Kentucky Fried Chicken, left school in seventh grade because of family poverty.

Harland Sanders was 10 years old when Ray Kroc was born in 1902, seemingly to be bored by school. "I liked action . . . I spent a lot of time thinking about things . . . for me, work was play," he said in his autobiography, *Grinding It Out* (St. Martin's Press, 1977). "My sophomore year in high school passed like a funeral . . . As school ended that spring, the United States entered World War I. I took a job selling coffee beans and novelties door-to-door. I was confident I could make my way in the world and saw no reason to return to school."

> **"My parents talked me into trying school again, but I lasted only one semester. Algebra had not improved in my absence." Ray Kroc went on to revolutionize fast-food service.**

This salesman managed to talk his parents into letting him become a Red Cross ambulance driver who was just about to leave for France when the armistice ended the war. "I went marching back home to Chicago," says Kroc, "wondering what to do next. My parents talked me into trying school again, but I lasted only one semester. Algebra had not improved in my absence." Kroc went on to revolutionize fast-food service with his chain of McDonald's restaurants.

One more friendly fast-food face left high school after tenth grade. R. David Thomas, better known as Dave Thomas, founded the Wendy's restaurant chain. Thomas left school because he knew he wanted to be in the restaurant business, and school just wasn't teaching him what he wanted or needed to know, he explains in his autobiography, *Dave's Way: A New Approach to Old Fashioned Success* (Putnam, 1991). In 1993, at the age of 60, Thomas studied for and got his General Equivalency Diploma (GED, equivalent to a high-school diploma).

A Few Other Homeschooled Business People and Entrepreneurs
> Andrew Carnegie—extremely wealthy steel manufacturer
> Soichiro Honda—creator of the Honda automobile company
> Jimmy Lai—newspaper publisher; founder of Giordano
>   International
> Joseph Pulitzer—newspaper publisher, established Pulitzer
>   Prize

Homeschooled Scientists and Inventors

The names of many homeschooled inventors are household words: Alexander Graham Bell, Eli Whitney, and Thomas Alva Edison. Edison (1847–1931) is a name homeschoolers seem to throw around more than the others. Maybe it's because so many homeschoolers can relate to the short Edison school experience.

When Mrs. Edison discovered not only that Thomas' schoolmaster hit his students with a leather strap, but had also called her little boy "addled," she ended his "formal" education after only three months, bringing him home to an environment where she made sure learning was fun and explorative. (She also furiously informed the schoolmaster that her son had "more sense in his little finger than you have in your entire body.") Mrs. Edison "bought him books full of experiments. He tested them enthusiastically, trying to prove the author wrong, and it became his life's passion. As one experiment led to another, he invented the telephone transmitter, stock ticker, mimeograph, phonograph, and perfected the electric light bulb," explains Ronald W. Clark in *Edison: The Man Who Made the Future* (Putnam, 1977).

Another homeschooler-turned-inventor is England's Michael Faraday (1791–1867) who is best known for work in electrochemistry. Faraday was "a poor boy, who like Tom (Edison) had never gone to school . . . Faraday, like Edison, had been poor and had been self-taught" (Margaret Cousins, *The Story of Thomas A. Edison,* Random House, 1965).

Bringing us up to modern times is inventor William Lear (1902–1978), creator of the airplane that bears his name—"a feisty, self-made millionaire who started life with only a grammar school education and a pocket full of tools, and yet produced many inventions," says Victor Boesen in *They Said It Couldn't Be Done: The Incredible Story of Bill Lear* (Doubleday, 1971).

> "Almost every day instead of going to school," said John James Audubon, "I usually made for the fields where I gathered bird's nests, eggs, lichens, flowers, and even pebbles."

"In high school," writes Boesen, "Lear corrected a statement his teacher made in electrical class one day, about an experiment with an ammeter. When the teacher challenged him to connect it the way he said was possible and it worked, his teacher told him, 'Since you're so smart, you won't need to come back to this class.'" After his physics and shop teachers did the same, Lear left school altogether.

John James Audubon (1785–1851) was an ornithologist also well known for his artistic talents. Here's what the *Dictionary of American Biographies* says about Audubon's homeschooling: "His father, occupied with the affairs of the Republic of France, left the supervision of the boy's studies to the boy's indulgent stepmother, with the result that the formal schooling was neglected." Audubon's own words reveal the direction his education took: "Almost every day instead of going to school, I usually made for the fields where I gathered bird's nests, eggs, lichens, flowers, and even pebbles"(Alexander B. Adams, *John James Audubon,* Putnam, 1966). Later in his life, Audubon cited his only memory of school as the time he got into a fight with a fellow student who hit Audubon with a rock and knocked him unconscious.

A Few Other Homeschooled Scientists and Inventors

John Moses Browning—firearms inventor and designer

Peter Cooper—invented skyscraper, built first U.S. commercial locomotive

Oliver Heaviside—physicist and electromagnetism researcher
Elias Howe—invented sewing machine
Cyrus McCormick—invented grain reaper
Guglielmo Marconi—developed radio
Sir Frank Whittle—invented turbo jet engine
Wilbur and Orville Wright—built first successful plane

Homeschooled Artists

Visual artists, writers, and performers are all well represented among the homeschooled "alumni." Their contributions to our society are highly valued.

> Mrs. Wright intended her son to be an architect even before he was born, and she hung engravings of cathedrals over the bed of young Frank Lloyd.

VISUAL ARTISTS

One of a whole family of artists, Charles Peale (1741–1827) "received the common rudiments of schooling until his thirteenth birthday, when he was apprenticed to a saddle maker," according to the *Dictionary of American Biographies*. Not only was Charles Peale homeschooled, he continued the tradition. "He believed anyone could learn to paint and taught many of his 17 children to paint" (*World Book Encyclopedia*, 1986).

Who taught Grandma Moses to paint? She did, and she did it in 1938, the year she turned 78. "Her father, who himself had artistic inclinations, encouraged the girl," reports James Kallir, author of *Grandma Moses: The Artist Behind the Myth* (Galerie, 1982). "Mother," explains the artist herself, "was more practical, thought I could spend my time in other ways." And so she did. After "briefly attending a one room district school," writes Kallir, "she hired out on a neighboring farm at 12, and managed all aspects of the household."

Mrs. Wright intended her son to be an architect even before he was born, and she hung engravings of cathedrals over the bed of young Frank Lloyd (1867–1959). The boy's early years were nomadic, as his father moved the family from place to place in search of a better job. By the time Frank was 11, he had lived in six towns and four states. "In his early teens, he worked summers to supplement family income, and when his parents divorced he left high school to take a job," reveals Richard C. Twombly in *Frank Lloyd Wright: His Life and Architecture* (Wiley, 1979). "He started college, but after two unproductive semesters, he moved to Chicago where he worked for three employers in a year. Despite . . . lack of formal training, Wright, by his mid-twenties, had acquired the social and architectural credentials necessary to become an upper middle class professional."

Photographer and conservationist Ansel Adams (1902–1984) grew up in the days when children like him were simply called "fidgety," rather than receiving the label of ADD (attention deficit disorder) or other learning disability. When Ansel's father saw that his son wasn't adjusting well to a school environment, he pulled him out of school to teach him at home. "[T]he next years were extremely fruitful," says writer Theresa Amabile. "Learning experiences were always tapped into the young boy's intrinsic interests, and ranged from playing the piano to visiting an exposition" (*Growing Up Creative,* Creative Education Foundation, 1992).

> "[Robert Frost's] first day of kindergarten was his last . . . Such schoolwork as he could be persuaded to do—and it was not much—he completed at home."

Adams best summarizes his own homeschooling, and his father's role in it: "I am certain he established the positive direction of my life that otherwise, given my native hyperactivity, could have been confused and catastrophic. I trace who I am and the direction of my development to those years of growing up in our house on the dune, propelled especially by an internal spark, tenderly kept alive and glowing, by my father" (*Growing Up Creative*).

A Few Other Homeschooled Artists
> William Blake
> Leonardo Da Vinci
> Claude Monet
> Andrew Wyeth

WRITERS

I can just imagine Nobel Prize–winning George Bernard Shaw telling an elegant crowd assembled to partake of his brand of wisdom, "My schooling not only failed to teach me what it professed to be teaching, but prevented me from being educated to an extent which infuriates me when I think of all I might have learned at home by myself" (Archibald Henderson, *George Bernard Shaw: Man of the Century,* Appleton-Century-Crofts, 1956).

Shaw may not have learned at home, but many other writers of note did, including Pulitzer Prize–winning poet Robert Frost (1874–1963) who showed early signs of a phenomenon related to compulsory school attendance, which is still common today. "On the first day of school, when Robbi made the strange journey, he felt unpleasantly lost before he had even reached the school, and the day was not half over when someone pushed him too high and too long on a backyard swing, with the result that he was sick to his stomach," explains biographer Lawrence Thomas in *Robert Frost—Early Years* (Henry Holt, 1982). "A further agony occurred when the omnibus driver on the home journey had so much difficulty finding Robbi's house that the boy wept for fear he would never see his mother again."

The next day, while getting ready for school, he developed a severe stomach pain and was permitted to stay at home. Since it worked well the first time, little Robbi used the same tactic over and over again. "[H]is first day of kindergarten was his last . . . Such schoolwork as he could be persuaded to do—and it was not much—he completed at home." Frost went on to pass a high-school entrance exam without any prior formal preparation.

Robert Frost was only a 1-year-old toddler when Samuel Clemens (1835–1910), pen name Mark Twain, was born. In one of his biographies about Clemens, Albert Bigalow Paine states, "He detested school as he detested nothing else on earth, even going to church" (*Mark Twain, A Biography: Vol. 1,* Harper & Bros., 1912).

Paine provides a bit more detail in *Boys Life of Mark Twain* (Harper & Bros., 1915–1916). Sam's father died when he was 11 years old. "Leading him into the room where his father lay, his mother said some comforting words, and asked him to make her a promise," Paine explains. "He flung himself into her arms, sobbing: 'I will promise anything if you won't make me go to school! Anything!' After a moment his mother said, 'No, Sammy, you need not go to school any more. Only promise me to be a better boy. Promise not to break my heart!'"

The biography notes for her novel *Death Comes for the Archbishop* reveal that Willa Cather (1873–1947) left Virginia society with her family as an 8-year-old to live on a Nebraska ranch. Here "she spent most of her time riding about on her pony, visiting her foreign-born neighbors." When she eventually entered high school, she "had read many of the English classics with her two grandmothers, and had learned Latin."

A turn-of-the-century English mother, Clara Christie, believed that children shouldn't read until they were 8 years old because it was better for both eyes and brain. Her homeschooling daughter, Agatha, couldn't wait, however, and "by the time she was 5, Agatha had taught herself to read by puzzling out a text that had often been told aloud to her . . . She had mastered reading by matching meaning to the appearance of entire words rather than by single letter . . . her spelling was always of the hit and miss sort," writes

> **"I am myself a product of homeschooling [until age 15]," says William F. Buckley Jr. "There were ten of us and life at home was as 'Life with Father' in the famous play, the father in question with a mad-dog enthusiasm for learning everything."**

Janet Morgan in *Agatha Christie* (Knopf, 1985). Agatha Christie (1890–1976) went on to spend only a couple of years in high school before becoming a world-renowned mystery writer.

Today, a homeschooler is the editor of the highly respected magazine *National Review* and has served for decades as a witty and respected voice of conservatism, both in print and television media. His name is William F. Buckley Jr. (born 1925), and in 1993 he wrote in his syndicated column, "On the Right": "I am myself a product of homeschooling [until age 15]. There were ten of us and life at home was as 'Life with Father' in the famous play, the father in question with a mad-dog enthusiasm for learning everything from Latin to how to construct ship models inside glass bottles."

William's father, Will Buckley Sr., preferred private tutors to sending his children to local schools. Other children in the neighborhood joined the Buckley offspring in the tutoring classroom. By the time they reached age 13, all the Buckley children were fluent in French, Spanish, and English (John B. Judis, "Famous Home Schoolers," *The Greenhouse Report,* October, 1990).

A Few Other Homeschooled Writers

Margaret Atwood
Noel Coward
Alex Haley
Sean O'Casey
Carl Sandburg
Walt Whitman
Laura Ingalls Wilder

PERFORMING ARTS

It was 1760 when 4-year-old homeschooler Wolfgang Amadeus Mozart learned to play the harpsichord. His father recognized amazing talent when he saw it, so "devoted most of his time to his son's general and musical education . . . Wolfgang never attended school" (*World Book Encyclopedia,* 1986). By the age of 14, he had already created an impressive portfolio of compositions.

Then there's the king of jazz, Louis Armstrong, born in 1898. Growing up in poverty, Louis was a homeschooler-by-default, working menial jobs and skipping school until "at 13 he was sent to reform school for firing a shot into the New Year's Day Parade," reports *Webster's American Biographies* (Merriam, 1974). It was "there he found a cornet and taught himself how to play it."

Child prodigy violinist Yehudi Menuhin (1916–1999) wrote about his homeschooling background in his autobiography, *Unfinished Journey:* "I went to school for precisely one day at the age of 6, by which time I could read quite well, and write, and calculate a little. My one day was not unhappy but bewildered," says Yehudi. "Very quietly I sat in the class, the teacher stood at the front and said incomprehensible things for a long time and my attention eventually wandered to the window through which I could see a tree. The tree was the only detail I remembered clearly enough to report at home that afternoon and that was the end of my schooling."

Not too many folks have missed hearing the voice of LeAnne Rimes, born in 1982 to become the teen-prodigy country singer who came onto the music scene like wildfire just a few years ago. LeAnne "dropped out of school to go on the road," reports *USA Weekend* writer Jennifer Mendelsohn (September 27–29, 1996). "She is homeschooled through Texas Tech University."

A Few Other Homeschooled Performing Artists

Irving Berlin—songwriter
Whoopi Goldberg—actress
Hanson—sibling singing group
Jennifer Love Hewitt—actress
Moffatts—Canada's version of Hanson
Frankie Muniz—actor

Homeschooled Military Personnel

> **More recent history finds George Patton learning at home, in part because he was dyslexic. "His parents kept him out of school. They were afraid that the taunts of classmates would sear his soul."**

An early homeschooler-turned-military-man is John Paul Jones (1747–1792), often called the father of the American Navy, but most remembered for his answer to a British demand that he surrender: "I have not yet begun to fight."

In *John Paul Jones* (Little, 1959), Samuel Eliot Morison writes "Early in 1761, at the age of 13, John packed a sea chest and embarked as a ship's boy on the brig *Friendship,* bound for Barbados. His formal schooling ended in 1759 at age 12."

More recent history finds George Patton (1885–1945) learning at home, in part because he was dyslexic. "His parents kept him out of school. They were afraid that the taunts of classmates would sear his soul," explains Martin Blumenson, author of *Patton: The Man Behind the Legend* (Morrow, 1986). "There was a strong bond between father and son. The father spent many hours reading to him and his sister . . . They let him express his high spirits however he could, and encouraged him to vent his frustrations in physical activity. The unbounded love of mamma and poppa, which provided him with self assurance, were the basic elements of Patton's ambition and achievement."

General Douglas MacArthur, born just one year after Patton, was taught by his mother until private tutors took over when he was 13. West Point welcomed him after he outscored everyone who had ever taken the entrance exam.

A Few Other Homeschooled Military Personnel

Senior Navy Officer John Barry—former head of the U.S. Navy

Commodore Matthew Perry—naval officer who opened up
    trade with Japan

General John Pershing—general of the armies of the United
    States

Admiral David Dixon Porter—Civil War commander

Homeschooled Politicians, Statesmen, and Jurists

I'm not at all surprised that the man who cried "Give me
Liberty or give me Death" was homeschooled in his childhood years.
Patrick Henry (1736–1799) grew into a revolutionary leader and
skilled orator, but he had "only the scantiest of schooling. His father
had given him some fundamental instruction in reading and arithmetic. His lessons took place mainly at home, at odd intervals, depending on the plantation routine. His 'formal' education ended when
he was 15, after his father had given him a course in Latin, some Greek,
and ancient history" (Henry Meyer, *A Son of Thunder: Patrick Henry
and the American Republic,* University Press of Virginia, 1992).

Homeschooler John Marshall (1755–1835) served as Chief
Justice of the Supreme Court from 1801 until his death. He "grew up
on his father's farm, and had little formal schooling," states the *World
Book Encyclopedia,* 1986. "Marshall became a lawyer in 1781, after
studying law on his own and attending some lectures at William &
Mary College."

Statesman Benjamin Franklin (1706–1790) spent 6 months
in school when he was 8 years old. After that, it was off to work in his
father's candle and soap shop and his half-brother's print shop. His first
essays were published when he was 16 years old, and one encyclopedia
states he taught himself to read French, Spanish, Italian, and Latin. A
strong presence in early American government, his inventive mind gave
us the Franklin stove and bifocals and his civic mind gave us volunteer
fire departments and the American Philosophical Society. His last public act was to ask Congress for the abolition of slavery.

Congressman Davy Crockett (1786–1836), better known as a frontiersman, didn't go to school until he was 13, and then, only for 4 days. "He left school after fighting with another boy, and ran away from home for 3 years to avoid punishment" (*World Book Encyclopedia,* 1986).

A Few Other Homeschooled Politicians, Statesmen, and Jurists

William Jennings Bryan—orator and statesman

Henry Clay—statesman

Alexander Hamilton—statesman and politician

Sam Houston—lawyer and first president of the Republic
of Texas

Chief Justice Charles Evans Hughes—jurist

Thomas Paine—political writer during the American
Revolution

> "At one school, [Mary Leakey] ate soap so that she would appear to be 'foaming at the mouth,' and she deliberately caused an explosion in chemistry class. After expulsion from two schools, Mary was educated at home."

A Few More Homeschooled Women of Note

It's interesting to see how many firsts, founders, feminists, and reformers appear when we visit historical women homeschoolers.

For starters, there's Susan B. Anthony (1820–1906), the reformer and women's rights leader. Susan could read and write at age 3. She went to a district school for a time before leaving it for the school her father created in their home for his own and neighbors' children. Early in her adult life, she spent a bit of time teaching in this school herself.

Homeschooler Florence Nightingale (1820–1910) was born in the same year as Susan B. Anthony. She did not attend school and was taught at home, predominantly by her father. At 34 years of age, Nightingale became a nurse to British troops during the war with Russia and went on to found the nursing profession as a result of her work.

Another homeschooled woman, Dr. Mary Walker (1832–1919), was a Civil War physician. The United States presented her a Congressional Medal of Honor in 1865; Dr. Walker was the only Civil War woman to receive one. How did this woman who became a woman's right advocate and physician spend her school years? "Her early education was obtained in the school conducted by her father, mother, and sisters on the family farm," explains the *Dictionary of American Biographies*. "She acquired the ambition to study medicine from her father. The rest of society disapproved of her ambition, her dress (trousers), and her doing man's work."

In the case of homeschooler Mary D. Leakey (1913–1996), her childhood is described as "a bit odd" (Lisa A. Lambert, *Pioneers: The Leakeys,* The Rourke Book Co., 1993). Mary grew up traveling through Europe as her father, a landscape artist, looked for scenes to paint. After her father died, Mary and her mother returned to England, where Mary was put into school for the first time.

"She did not adjust well to the restrictions of life at the different schools she briefly attended," writes biographer Lisa Lambert. "At one school, she ate soap so that she would appear to be 'foaming at the mouth,' and on another occasion she deliberately caused an explosion in chemistry class. After expulsion from two schools, Mary was educated at home by her mother or tutors."

Mary grew up to become a well-known "fossil hunter," and, with her husband, Richard Leakey, made major contributions to our understanding of early human ancestors. On December 9, 1996, the day Mary Leakey passed away, National Public Radio reviewed her accomplishments. After Richard Potts, director of the Smithsonian Institution's Human Origins project, recited a most impressive list,

> **As you can see from these stories, the homeschooling spirit, far from being a modern phenomenon, has thrived for a long time.**

reporter Charlayne Hunter-Gault asked him, "And yet she never—she wasn't a trained scientist, was she?"

Potts replied, "No, but she always had a great love for the origin of things, for discoveries about pre-history, and also for drawing, drawing of stone artifacts, of cave paintings, which she greatly admired and enjoyed work on in East Africa, and that gave her a tremendous degree of skill in observation and in detail."

A Few Other Homeschooled Women of Note

Abigail Adams—distinguished and influential first lady; wife of U.S. President John Adams; mother of President John Quincy Adams

Elizabeth Blackwell—first woman in the United States to receive a medical degree

Jill Ker Conway—historian and first woman president of Smith College

Gloria Steinem—founder and long-time editor of *Ms.* magazine

Frances E. C. Willard—educator, temperance leader, and suffragist

Tying It All Together

As you can see from these stories, the homeschooling spirit, far from being a modern phenomenon, has thrived for a long time. In the 150 years since the inception of compulsory school attendance, a sizeable number of American citizens received their education outside of this compulsion.

Today, homeschoolers represent an estimated 2% of all school-age children, and the percentage is increasing steadily. Today, it is not as difficult as it has been over the last few decades to find adults who have spent some of their compulsory school-age years outside of school.

Our brief homeschooling history tour has shown us that from the past into the present homeschooling has served both the individuals who participated in it and the society they joined as adults very well. Now let's take a look at the lives of some contemporary men and women who have also spent time growing in freedom and liberated from compulsory school attendance.

I

The Adults

My favorite thing *to do was wander through the woods and fill up my pockets and little bags with nuts and rocks and sticks. We have boxes and boxes in our attic just labeled "Jed's Nature Stuff." I loved fossils. I'd go through our driveway gravel looking for shell fragments. I collected feathers, mosses, and big buckets of frogs' eggs from the pond and creek.*

2

A Cultural Rip Van Winkle

JEDEDIAH PURDY

Born: November 29, 1974; Chloe, West Virginia

Homeschooling: Birth to 1988

Family: Parents—Walter and Deirdre; Siblings—Charles (34), Hannah (23)

Most memorable wisdom about life or learning: My mother told me that the point of writing is to have something to say. My father said to try to take a small corner of the world and make it as sane as possible.

Favorite study: Early years—amateur naturalism and the sciences; Teen years—political and social issues

Current Work: Yale University Law School (class of 2001)

He's a Yale University law student. He's also the author of a new book capturing a storm of media attention. Among the media compelled to offer their views on his book *For Common Things: Irony, Trust, and Commitment in America Today* are *Time, Salon, Harper's,* the *New York Times Magazine,* and National Public Radio news. The young man has taken the time to give an interview to each. Still, Jedediah (Jed) Purdy is pleasantly accessible and accommodating of yet another interview, this one with a homeschooling mom.

In an October 24, 1999, *Special to the Washington Post* piece entitled "The Adventures of Anti-Irony Boy," journalist Katherine Marsh wrote that homeschooler Jed "has been portrayed as a cultural Rip Van Winkle with his idealism miraculously intact. As the story goes, Purdy's parents forsook the outside world, moved to the wilds of Chloe, West Virginia, and brought up Purdy and his sister in barn-raising utopian bliss."

Well, that's *part* of the story. Mom Deirdre, an attorney raised in an affluent Delaware family, has over the years found herself involved in local educational politics and state-level homeschooling issues, working as a real estate abstracter and more recently as a court reporter. She takes us to what just may be the beginning of the story of how Jed Purdy became a homeschooling folktale at the age of 24.

Destined for Homeschooling

"I feel like I was so lucky," says Deirdre about, of all things, the rheumatic fever she contracted when she was 7 years old. "I was in second grade and I didn't have to go to school for almost the entire year. Instead, my father brought me lots of books from the library and I just read and read and read. When I went back to school, I knew much more than the students who were in school. The only thing I had missed was borrowing in subtraction which was not a big thing to make up."

"It gave me a perspective on this whole thing that there really wasn't much going on in school," Deirdre continues. "What I read about and learned when I was home carried me through high school. I also remember being so bored because the school had to cater to the lowest common denominator. I knew there wasn't anything going on there that was magical or necessary."

Deirdre harbored no doubts that someday, if she ever had children of her own, they would grow without compulsory-attendance school. Dad Wally recalls the couple's introduction to the actual word "homeschooling."

"A supplement to the *Whole Earth Catalog* had a little blip about homeschooling pioneer John Holt's newsletter, no more than a paragraph or two," he says. "This made so much sense we sent off for the newsletter right away. It sounded right right off the bat." Homeschooling was also perfectly legal in West Virginia at the time, if only under a legal loophole—an existing exemption that allowed families to file as private schools.

> **"I remember being so bored because the school had to cater to the lowest common denominator."**

Jed knew early on why he wasn't stepping on to a school bus each weekday. "Our parents had this strong idea that schools were regimenting and stifling, that people just sat there all day listening to someone at the front of the room. They didn't want us to do that," he says. Jed liked the idea of learning at home. Other neighbors began to like it, too, and a small but supportive homeschooling community blossomed in Chloe.

Homeschooling in the Purdy household relied less on formal curriculum and much more on life rhythms. Long before Jed began reading "seriously" around 6 years old, his parents, especially Wally, "would read to us almost every night for an hour or two," he says. "We went through *The Chronicles of Narnia,* biographies of historical figures, T. H. White's *The Sword and the Stone.* I remember waiting to be able to read with a keen eagerness because the read-aloud sessions were never enough. I wanted to be able to read all day because it was so fantastic," says Jed. "*Charlotte's Web* was the first book I read to myself."

Together, Jed and his sister, Hannah, discovered the *Star Wars* phenomenon through a Public Radio production instead of at the local movie theater. "There was a dramatization of the J. R. R. Tolkien series which was also fantastic," Jed adds. "We loved those programs."

> "Mostly homeschooling and life were about reading and being outdoors; that was the structure of our education."

Arithmetic lessons irregularly entered Jed and Hannah's day once a week for an hour or so. "Mom generally, but sometimes Dad, would introduce us to basic concepts, like [the algebraic] *x*. Other than that, we would get up and often one or both of us would spend a good part of the day reading whatever was around for 4, 5, 6 hours," Jed says. "Sometimes I'd be in a very intense project trying to read everything the Charleston library had on the history of the Celtic regions of Europe, or werewolves, or maybe reading casually through a stack of old Hardy Boys novels from the thrift store."

The day didn't end there. "Very often at some point I would go off on a long hike, maybe much of the day, just following ridges and creek beds to see where I would end up. Or a little later, about the time I got to be 11 or 12 years old, I'd go off for a bicycle ride for the day just following back roads, sometimes with a friend, sometimes alone. I had a good, good friend who lived nearby and we often did things together. I'd wait for him to get home from school, we'd do it on weekends, or he'd 'take off' a day."

Growing up on a rural West Virginia farm also meant incorporating chores into daily activity. "I would often walk up the hill to the cattle barn," Jed explains, "clean out the stalls, give them hay or salt, or do something similar for the horses whose barn was up a different slope in a different direction. In the evenings, we'd generally read again. Mostly homeschooling and life were about reading and being outdoors; that was the structure of our education."

Changes

Television entered the Purdy home when Jed was about 10 years old, a year when, according to Jed, the World Series was "especially enticing" to the men he knew. He laughs as he calls that World Series "the source of a lot of backsliding in our community." Even though the TV became a permanent household fixture, it came late enough in Jed and Hannah's lives to prevent them from "developing the idea that TV would be a reflexive way of entertaining ourselves. When we had 10 minutes and a snack, we'd sit down with a newspaper or a book or a magazine."

Also when Jed was a 10-year-old, the modern homeschooling movement was experiencing a boom, and some West Virginia legislators decided to try to revise the private school exemption to exclude families, that is, homeschoolers. Deirdre explains, "In the legislators' minds, homeschooling wasn't going to happen. The existing law allowed homeschooling, but it had never occurred to them that it would be used this way. They thought school would be 'school.' When our local superintendent threatened to put us in jail, well, that was an impetus to go to the legislature."

When the legislature went into session that year, the Purdys, along with other homeschooling families, visited the capitol several days each week. "We went down in complete naivete," says Deirdre. "Our wonderful children were there, and we had Jed speak to the legislature." A bill was passed that at least created a couple of rather burdensome options to provide breathing space to families who wanted to educate their children in this way. Deirdre admits some homeschooling problems continue today because of compromises made and circumstances unconsidered. The required annual standardized testing and minimum score requirements remain problems for West Virginia families with special needs children.

The requirement that a homeschooling parent possess 4 years more of formal education than the most academically advanced child being homeschooled closed the homeschooling door to some families. Thanks to recent efforts by the state's homeschoolers, the West Virginia legislature agreed to drop this requirement for a year while they conduct a study to verify homeschoolers' claims that a child's educational success isn't tied to a parent's formal education.

In Chloe, West Virginia, opportunities to volunteer at soup kitchens or in tutoring programs were not available, as they are to homeschoolers living in more populated areas. Instead, Jed says, "You take a neighbor some corn. We worked with others by going to do whatever they were doing. When a neighbor was blacksmithing, he would let us hang out and beat on the metal. Working with others often meant helping in their gardens or putting up hay, but that was just visiting, and what people did when they visited."

As a young teenager, many of Jed's visits led to neighbor Bill Howley, a Yale-graduate-turned-farmer, homeschooling father, and "somewhat of an amateur political economist," says Jed. "Bill gave me lectures on political economy while I helped him put up hay. The discipline of talking to someone who was a skeptic, even a cynic, helped me a lot. Bill didn't believe in the good intentions of politicians, executives, or celebrities. He taught me that to understand an institution or a society, you had to know who held power, what kind of power, and over whom. It was like putting up hay with a hardened journalist whose beat was the world."

Jed's interest was turning toward political and social issues. "Around that time we had an issue of the *New Yorker* lying around," Jed recalls. "There was a one-column squib—utterly random—on various theories of what capitalism would come to in the end; Adam Smith's theory, Karl Marx' theory, and others. I looked at them, and for the next week I carried them around in my head, referred to them, cycled through them to see if I could remember the points of each. It was just beautiful to think about the whole structure of society and what's going to come of it. That and the hayfield lectures were decisive moments in getting interested in the kind of thing that I've more recently been interested in."

Eventually, some of the local homeschooling families moved away, shrinking the already small source of support. Deirdre began working outside the home more often. Wally, who had previously farmed full time, began not-quite-full-time work as a timber frame carpenter. "This meant there was less going on at home day in and day out," says Jed. His thoughts, and Hannah's, turned to school attendance.

> "School was boring and enormously inefficient, and it was scarcely learning."

A couple of months into the ninth grade year (sixth grade for Hannah), Jed entered government school and stayed through his junior year. "It was boring and enormously inefficient, and it was scarcely learning," Jed acknowledges. "It was rote and dulling and, with the exception of a couple of very good teachers, I and other students who were any good essentially taught ourselves."

During the first year of school attendance, Jed felt socially inept because he had no sense of what the school's socialization rules were or how he would be judged. "I fit in through acclimation, just getting the hang of it." He adds, "I never cared for it, though." As for socializing with the ladies, Jed claims homeschooling didn't interfere. "I'm plenty capable of interfering with that on my own."

In the meantime, Jed's half-brother, Charles, was teaching at New Hampshire's private Phillips Exeter Academy. Jed never forgot an earlier visit to the school, nor his brother's invitation to consider Exeter if he ever wanted to leave West Virginia. Jed decided to apply to the school for his senior year. Not only wasn't his homeschooling background a problem, "I think they considered it an asset if anything," he says.

"Exeter was educationally wonderful," Jed remembers. "It was run around a seminar system. There was a lot of back and forth. The teachers were in some cases extremely skillful and effective at drawing insights out of the children. It was ideal for me at that stage of life."

From Exeter it was on to travel in eastern Europe and work as a carpenter back home in West Virginia. In 1993, Jed enrolled in Harvard (another school that appreciated Jed's former homeschooling learning style), and today he's in Yale Law School. There he's sprinkling the law program with courses in philosophy, as well as environmental issues through a few courses at forestry school. Generous financial aid and scholarships, including the federal government's Truman Scholarship, helped make all the private schooling possible. The $75,000 advance and future royalties from *For Common Things* should help, too.

The young writer shares some of his homeschooling story in the pages of that first book whose main point, in Katherine Marsh's words, "is an impassioned plea for renewed commitment to, and belief in, grassroots politics as a way to improve the world." In Jed's words, this commitment requires "a way of thinking, and doing, that has more promise of goodness than the one we are now following."

Looking Back and Reaching Forward

Jed acknowledges that it's impossible to know how things would have turned out differently for his parents' lives if they had not practiced homeschooling, but he notes that, "Probably homeschooling tends to make you a political skeptic. My parents are both basically liberal people politically—how they vote, how they feel about a range of social and political issues. Homeschooling definitely puts you on the wrong side of liberal platitude and introduces you first-hand to a lot of bureaucratic silliness and a lot of unconvincing sanctimony about the public schools because you sort of see what they're not doing."

"I think the experience was instructive in the sense that it put them on the 'outside' and made them political allies with fundamentalist Christians in the state. That was certainly not our ethos. I wouldn't say we left our differences behind, but we found some interesting common ground. Homeschooling was probably very shoring in those ways and in the sense of shaking up your bottom mud a little."

Deirdre and Wally skip the politics and go straight to the heart about homeschooling's impact on their lives. "We have a really close family," says Deirdre. "Absolutely," Wally adds quickly. He must be quick; Deirdre isn't anywhere near finished on this topic.

"We're close because we had so much time together," she continues. "There are all those years you go to the store, your children are with

> "There are all those years you go to the store, your children are with you. You go to the post office, your children are with you because you're homeschoolers."

you. You go to the post office, your children are with you because you're homeschoolers. People I talk to don't understand what they're missing; they have no idea. I remember when Jed and Hannah went to school for the first time. I was by myself for the first time in 12 years. On one hand it was nice; very quiet and nobody fighting in the back seat. I could go wherever I wanted. But it made me realize all that time we had all been together. All parents seem to feel the same when their kids go off to school, but most of the time they're so much younger. They really haven't had all that shared experience."

Jed recognizes that his early learning lifestyle still influences how he learns today. "Neither Hannah nor I had as our first encounter with education the experience of tasks being placed on us from outside that *might* interest us," he begins. "That would more likely be just keeping us from doing whatever it was we were actually interested in."

What effect did freedom to choose their own learning tasks based on personal interests have on the siblings? "One effect was that we were fairly easily excited about learning and often able to find a topic in a book or a course later in life that *did* excite us, identify it as interesting, and go with it because that's the sort of thing we had always done. That's what learning had been. On the other hand—and while this isn't bad, it can be inconvenient—we have a little less patience for being put through work we find tedious or frustrating. I'm afraid I developed a thicker skin for that than might be good in public school in West Virginia, and a bit in law school as well."

"Generally speaking," Jed summarizes, "we both tend to follow our interests and make a lot of connections that aren't necessarily obvious or conventional, but come out of the way a topic interests us or out of other things we've cared about. People come to that attitude in different ways, and homeschooling is certainly not a necessary condition for getting there, but it was our way to get there."

If Jed ever has little Purdys running around in the future, they, too, are likely to learn at home. "I want them to delight in learning and have a sense of control over and responsibility for their own decisions about what they learn and what they do. I'd like them to be integrated into their parents' work and a larger community. I'd much rather that than have a community made up mostly of people all born within a year of each other."

Jed graduates from Yale law school in 2001. He foresees "some work as an attorney in the short run." In the bigger picture, though, life's work is filled with limitless possibilities. "It will be a combination of teaching, writing, and doing public work, probably in the areas of environment and human rights," he says. Jed plans to pursue his interests in legal reform and the design of international standards for the environment, labor conditions, and subsequent enforcement mechanisms. The only question is how. "Whether teaching, teaching law, teaching something else as the main thing; whether working at some sort of nonprofit or think-tank organization; whether something else entirely, I'm not sure."

While Jed may be unclear as to the exact route he will travel, past examination of lives he admires has clarified *how* he will proceed. "When I think about the sort of life I'd like to have, it has very much to do with being clear about the activities and things about the natural world and social world that you think are good, being able to feel that you're doing some justice to those things; preserving them, enhancing them, just being around them, both in your work and in the way your private life and your family life are formed," he says. The continuity between values, work, and beliefs that is important to Jed will guide him into the future.

"I think that's a lot of what homeschooling was all about," Jed notes, "wanting to be able to believe in your life and have it all more or less, if not in one place—though that was often true— then at least within a continuous frame of activity and thinking and caring. In that sense, the sort of life that I admire and would like to have has a good deal in common with the sort of life that homeschooling was an attempt to achieve."

> "The sort of life that I admire and would like to have has a good deal in common with the sort of life that homeschooling was an attempt to achieve."

The homeschooling experience touched every member of the Purdy family, and its benefits permeate their lives even today. The results have inspired Deirdre and Wally—as so many other homeschooling parents—to offer encouraging words to today's young families. Homeschool advocacy is often a challenge, though, because the actual experience of homeschooling moves beyond any possible description of it.

Deirdre echoes many a homeschooling advocate's frustration at times. "I get discouraged by how many people who really care about their children—their lifestyle, what they eat, where they live, all these things—dismiss the idea of homeschooling by saying it's too hard, it's going to interfere with my career, things you would *never* expect them to say. They put up artificial barriers just so they can go on doing whatever they're doing. You can't run them down by saying, 'Oh, you're slighting your children.' Then the ones who are truly interested in homeschooling get all the pressures that we got—your children won't be socialized, you don't know what you're doing. It's hard to give [parents] that needed courage."

Yet there's a secret almost universally recognized by homeschooling parents that, despite the frustration, keeps Deirdre trying. "Nothing can replace children's desire to learn," she says. "Certainly no amount of money, blackboards, or materials can replace children wanting to learn, and they mostly don't in schools. It's almost beaten out of them. If their teachers don't make it really uninteresting, their peers make it undesirable."

"I think homeschooling is about trust, and maybe the hardest thing is to trust your kids and to trust yourself to be able to do right by them."

Jed aims his advice about homeschooling at those parents who worry about whether they are competent enough. "They seem to think there's some kind of trick or you have to be really amazing. Or they think their kids have to be amazing," he says. "None of that seems really right. The basic idea of homeschooling as we did it was that if you trust the kids, treat them well, and provide a solid enough model for them, *it will work out!* There may be a year when their percentile ranking on the standardized test that the state asks them to take worries you. There may be a year when you think that they're behind in reading. There may be 6 months when you feel like they're just poking around with an Erector set and not advancing and you worry. But I think it's about trust, and maybe the hardest thing is to trust your kids and to trust yourself to be able to do right by them. The evidence is starting to suggest that it works out."

"So that's it," Jed concludes. "Don't worry too much about the mechanics and don't worry too much about qualifications. If you have the desire to do it and you're not psychopathic, you can probably do it very well."

EARLIER THIS YEAR, *when all the media was bothering me, several people after the interviews told me that I was not their typical representation of someone who's supposed to be "smart." I've always taken that as a compliment.*

3

1600: Reaching Academic Perfection

MONIQUE HARRIS

Born: June 25, 1981; born Little Rock, Arkansas
Homeschooling: 1986–1996; 1998–1999
Family: Parents—George and Rhonda; Sibling—Mark (8)
Most memorable wisdom about life or learning: From Mom—Education is something too many people take lightly; from Dad—What I study is my choice.
Favorite study: Early years—reading; Middle years—science, nature, reading; Teen years—math, creative writing, biology
Current Work: Student at John Brown University (class of 2003)

Monique's homeschooling kindergarten began after dark when mom Rhonda returned home from full-time work as a certified public accountant, and dad George took off his tie after a long day as chief fiscal officer for Arkansas' Department of Human Services. Monique's best friend, a year older than she, was a homeschooler, and the child's parents had encouraged Rhonda and George. Coupled with some preliminary research on homeschooling, Rhonda decided the challenge of combining work and homeschooling would be worth the effort.

She soon saw the benefits of homeschooling for her daughter, so the following year Rhonda left her job, and mother and daughter dived into the world of phonics and the *Noah Webster Blue-Back Speller*. "That thing is the most boring thing in the entire world," Monique states emphatically. She much more enjoyed the weekly piano lessons with their pastor's wife that began around the same time.

When she was 8 years old and already a reader for 3 years, each week Monique borrowed five Nancy Drew books from the library. And Beverly Cleary. And biographies, especially ones about Native Americans. She figures she probably read the Bible three times before she was a teenager.

As a pre-teen, Monique found herself drawn to the ideas of science and nature. Although she didn't feel she had very much control over her education during these years, Monique realizes her mom "gently and slowly turned over the reins to me starting in about seventh grade. Then," she says, "the only thing we did together was math; I self-studied everything else. She would make the lesson plans and give me a schedule by which I would have to get the tests done."

Monique's years of piano lessons became the source of self-employment when she realized there was no one in her town to teach two girls who wanted to learn how to play. "As a sophomore I started with those two students; by my senior year I had 11," Monique says. "I was pretty cheap as far as teachers go. I was in it a little bit for the money, but also because I love to teach people things. I loved to watch the girls grow in their knowledge of music. I charged $6 for a half-hour lesson. I figured making $12 an hour in high school was pretty good."

Temporary Detour

When her homeschooling friend decided to attend school, so did Monique. "At this point I was more aware that I was 'missing out' on the day-in, day-out socialization, and more and more friends who went to public school were asking, 'Man, how can you stand to be by yourself every day?' I don't know if I would have had those thoughts if others hadn't brought them up to me."

Monique entered Abundant Life, a Christian high school a 40-minute commute away, as a sophomore. She remembers well her first history test. "Our teacher gave us a review before the first test," says Monique. "I thought the review was just some questions to help us out. I wrote them all down. He gave us some names and who they were and I wrote that down, too. I studied that, plus all my other notes that night. The next day I found out the 'review' *was* the test! Here I had studied until I knew the chapter backwards and forwards. I was expecting it to be a lot harder."

> **"Everything but science and math was either stuff I already knew or stuff I could have figured out on my own without spending 45 minutes listening to someone lecture."**

"They didn't give us any kind of responsibility to learn the materials ourselves, with the exception of science and math, and I did appreciate my school experience for those subjects," Monique says. "But everything else was either stuff I already knew or stuff I could have figured out on my own without spending 45 minutes in a class listening to someone lecture over it."

The school gave Monique credit for the challenging academic track she pursued during many years of homeschooling in the form of four-point credits, or A's. But the school used a grading system in which five-point credits were awarded for an A in a harder class. When she entered the school, Monique had been assured that her true grade-point average would be reflected by the time she became a senior.

At the close of her junior year, however, Monique saw that despite hard work and "blowing away everybody else in my class on every subject but history and Bible, I was going to be fourth in the class after never having made a B in my entire life," she says. The family appealed to the superintendent but got nowhere.

"I sort of lost my purpose for wanting to excel," Monique recalls. "I'd always wanted to get a 104 on a test. Now I thought, 'What's the use if I can work *not* very hard and be in the same position in my class?' I knew I didn't have a chance of actually getting what I'd been working toward for 2 years. I figured I'd be miserable if I stayed there."

This wasn't the only aspect of schooling with which Monique was disillusioned. "I expected more of what I'm getting in college right now. I expected stricter teachers, harder material, and I guess I expected, because it was a Christian school, that everyone would act like a Christian."

Monique came back home for her senior year of high school. She continued to work hard during the first semester, completing study of economics, American literature, and physics at home, and taking psychology and Western Civilization classes at Central Baptist College in Conway, Arkansas. In the second semester, she had only calculus and Greek left to go at home, so she grabbed an opportunity to volunteer with the Arkansas Family Council in Little Rock (the state capital) for 3 days each week from January to May.

Since George works at the capitol building, Monique's volunteer job allowed the two more time together than they had before, sharing commuting time and occasional lunches.

"I also wanted to see more of how government works," Monique comments. "My responsibilities included secretarial work and filing House and Senate bills. During the morning, I sat in House education committee on Tuesday and Thursday, and the Senate education committee on Wednesday. I took notes, briefed the council members on what was going on, what bills were up, or called them from wherever they were when a surprise bill came up and they needed to address it."

Acing the SATs

The state of Arkansas, like some other states, more often uses the ACT (American College Test) college entrance exam than the SAT (Scholastic Assessment Test). Indeed, Monique notes a newspaper report that in a previous year, 20,000 Arkansas high school seniors took the ACT, while only 2,000 took the SAT.

Monique faced the ACT exam four times, beginning in ninth grade, improving her score each time until on the third attempt she hit the magic score 32 (of 36), entitling her to receive the Governor's Distinguished Scholarship. "It covers everything," says Monique, "tuition, room, board, and fees. The only thing it doesn't cover is books."

At the time, Monique wasn't aware that she would receive yet another state scholarship to cover books and incidentals, so she decided to take the SAT exam to advance further in the National Merit Scholarship program. "Well that, and the prestige of the whole thing," she adds. In October of her senior year, Monique set her sights on becoming a National Merit Scholarship semi-

> **Monique faced the ACT exam four times, and on the third attempt she hit the magic score 32 (of 36), entitling her to receive the Governor's Distinguished Scholarship.**

finalist as she sat down in a big lecture hall sparsely populated with fellow test-takers.

> **Monique had attained the highest SAT score possible—1600.**

She was well prepared. "I got a great big book that had in it ten actual SAT tests that had been given before," she explains. "I went through all of those so when I actually took the test it was my eleventh time. I also went through the Princeton Review, which was really funny. They treat the exam as if it's a really light subject and give some advice on how to look through the questions in a way in which you don't really have to know everything they're talking about. You just have to know how to eliminate the wrong answers.

"This is the technique I used," Monique notes. "I would never pick out the right answer. I would cross off all the ones I knew were wrong. Usually I ended up with one answer. Sometimes I'd end up with two and then I'd read over the question again and answer what sounded best."

Weeks later, after a typical day attending college classes, Monique returned home looking forward to that evening's Harvest Carnival festivities. Rhonda came out of the house as soon as she heard Monique's car. She was holding the still-sealed envelope they both knew contained Monique's test score. "I read it and I thought, 'No, this isn't mine. This is an example of something to show you how to read your score or something like that,'" she remembers. "After I read it over a few times, though, I started dancing and hopping around my car for at least 5 minutes. Mom jumped right along with me!"

Monique had attained the highest SAT score possible—1600. As a side benefit, Monique received a life lesson in media attention, learning to handle reporters who knew "Homeschooler Scores Perfect 1600 on SAT" would give them an attention-grabbing headline.

A Head Start and
a Double Major

While attending the orientation program at Central Baptist College, Monique discovered that if she could pass an initial test she would receive six credits for both Old and New Testament survey without actually sitting through the courses. Folks told her nobody ever passed the test but Monique saw no harm in seeing how well she could do. When she did pass, "the nice thing about it was that John Brown University [in Siloam Springs, Arkansas], the school I planned to attend, would accept the credits," she says. She received even more credits for the two courses she took while still in "homeschooling high school."

But Monique wasn't finished yet. At church one day, she learned about CLEP tests, short for College Level Examination Program. It's a "college credits by exam" program, currently administered by more than 2,800 U.S. colleges and universities. Through the program, students can demonstrate they possess college-level knowledge no matter how they got it, whether through independent study, life experience, cultural pursuits, or other avenue. In this way, students can save time *and* money. Monique opted for English (3 credits), college algebra (3 credits), and Spanish (6 credits) CLEP tests. By traveling just 20 miles to a college that administered the CLEP, Monique acquired 24 credits after a few tests and physical attendance in just two college classes.

Monique calls the 24-credit head start "a typical light year." This eager college student is a double major whose semesters are closer to 30 to 36 credits (15 to 17 credits per semester is a common freshman load). She's working on two bachelor of arts degrees—music with emphasis on piano, and English with emphasis on teaching English to speakers of other languages (TESOL).

This isn't quite the path Monique originally set out on. She'd been in John Brown University for 2 weeks as an English and biology major when "I realized I loved playing piano enough to study it in college," she says. "I'd been doing a lot of thinking about it over the summer, about how much I enjoyed it, but at first it was going to be something I'd just do on the side while I pursued something else. If I had to buckle down and *really* practice to become a music major, I thought, 'I can do this for hours. I never would want to leave my practice room.'"

> **Monique had been in John Brown University for 2 weeks as an English and biology major when she "realized I loved playing piano enough to study it in college."**

Against her advisor's counsel, Monique proceeded to try to drop Biology I and Chemistry I to take music classes instead, even though she figured she'd have to wait until the end of the semester to accomplish it. "But the music teachers let me in their classes and I was able to arrange my schedule around it. They thought they were out of books for a music theory class, but one girl dropped out of the program 2 days before my decision to be in it and I had my book. Everybody was amazed." Monique worked hard to make up the 4 weeks she was now behind her classmates while keeping up the 9 hours a week practice schedule that continues.

"I've been classically trained so I do classical music lessons now because the college doesn't have a sacred music degree. What I really enjoy is hymn and praise song arranging. I'm going to have some classes that will teach advanced composing and arranging which might include hymns. I find that as I get better at classical music and at expression, my hymn arranging and ability to improvise gets better, too. Hopefully that will remain true throughout college."

Monique intends to finish college and enter the ministry. "I don't know whether or not that's going to be as a pastor's wife or a missionary," she says, weighing her options. "As a missionary it would be useful to have something to take overseas as an occupation; I can use music in a lot of areas. I've narrowed the field of people that I date to those going into the ministry, and the fellow I'm with right now plans to be a pastor or a missionary so it's worked out pretty well." This is the same fellow who had the misfortune of hoping to impress Monique with his SAT scores when they met at a scholarship weekend.

Since then, Monique has seen a lot of him, though not on many formal dates, according to her view. "Dates are usually things planned in advance where the guy takes the girl out to dinner kind of thing. We've only really had officially two dates if that's how you define dates. We're just with each other all the time at school, hanging out, talking to other friends. We don't do a lot of things alone; we like to be around other people. We get together, play the guitar and piano, things like that."

Time for Self

Like others, Monique credits her homeschooling experience with giving her self-motivation. "I don't have to have people spoon-feed me things. I can go out and learn things I need to know myself," she says. "That's helped a lot in college, because people I've met there have gotten a real shock when they're used to getting spoon-fed."

Homeschooling is also recognized as the source of this college student's sense of individuality. "I don't identify with a certain peer group, and I don't define my worth as a person by what my peer group thinks of me," Monique explains. "I only really began to appreciate homeschooling after attending a Christian school. I think it's made me more inclined to homeschool my own family if and when I have one. Spiritually, the two roughest years I had were the ones at school because I didn't have any time to do anything. With homeschooling, I felt I could take my Bible out in the woods, sit on a rock, and read it for hours. The Bible and time for me—that is what has given me the perspective on life that I have now."

Time for Monique has helped her to refine her definition of success. "Success for me would be becoming the woman God wants me to be, whatever that is," she begins. "I'm endeavoring. I'm going to college to try to learn more, expand my mind, and answer questions about why I believe what I believe so I'll be better equipped during the rest of my life to endeavor to do that."

> "Homeschooling has had an impact on my thinking about that prevalent attitude. Those letters [M.D.] after my name really don't matter to me anymore."

Homeschooling—and its gift of time—played a role in the formulation of this definition. "In school, the idea is that success is dependent on many worldly ideas; it's making a lot of money or becoming prestigious," Monique says. "I got caught up in it, too. The prevalent attitude is 'Being a wife and mother is going to waste your talents.' I was planning on going into medicine. That was actually, sadly, one of my motivations— I thought it would be cool to be Monique Harris, M.D. But having homeschooled, and having had my mom, who easily could have made money and a name for herself, choose to homeschool, has had an impact on my thinking about that prevalent attitude. Those letters after my name really don't matter to me anymore."

AUTHOR'S NOTE: At press time, Monique's life journey has changed course once more. She's planning to graduate with a bachelor of arts in music and a bachelor of science in psychology. She's "working to get as many hours out of the way as I can in preparation for the possibility of attending Oxford during a portion of my junior year."

I DIDN'T LEARN *to read until I was 13, just didn't have the desire to. My sister would read to us, so we didn't need to read. We'd go off and pick berries for jam and my other brother would go hunting. The biggest thing was training a stallion to ride when all the old farmers said I couldn't do it. He was the gentlest riding horse. He didn't have a name really, we just called him The Stallion.*

4

My Parents Weren't Going to Let Anybody Stop Them

AARON TIMLIN

Born: March 1, 1971; Detroit, Michigan

Homeschooling: 1979–1984

Family: Parents—Hugh Timlin and Sandra Two Moons; Siblings—Jacob (28), Rebekah (26), Daniel (24), Rachel (21), Mara (19), Joseph (17)

Most memorable wisdom about life or learning: From Dad—Be in charge of the direction of your own life; From Mom—A healthy diet = a healthy mind.

Favorite study: Early years—playing in the sandbox, casting on Dad's potter's wheel; Middle years—making wine, riding horses, acting; Teen years—theater, writing

Current work: Owner and director of Detroit Contemporary Art Gallery (since 1998); GyroDesign Web-site curator; apartment building manager

A 1981 move from the suburbs of Dearborn, Michigan, to an isolated, self-sufficient farm marked the early days of the Timlin family's homeschooling experience. Harsh Michigan winters often left parents and siblings snowed in for weeks at a time. Just the thought of this might be enough to push today's busy parents over the edge, but when daily activity centers around meaningful life essentials anyway, and there's nothing tugging your thoughts toward something "out there" that you may be missing, it's an adventure enjoyed by all. In fact, it's an adventure that builds a family viewed by others as a tightly knit clan.

From City to Country

The Vietnam War was raging while Hugh Timlin studied for the Catholic priesthood. It wasn't long, though, before he dropped out of the seminary because of a difference of opinion with the church's position on sending seminarians to fight the war.

> The Waldorf educational approach, with its emphasis on the arts, helped make the transition to home-schooling a smooth one.

Hugh turned sculptor and instructor at the Society for Arts & Crafts (now called the Center for Creative Studies) in Dearborn. He married Sandra, a weaver, and soon had a young and rapidly growing family settled in the suburbs. Their oldest child, Aaron, briefly attended kindergarten at the same elementary school his father had. From there, Aaron was off to Detroit Waldorf School through third grade, followed closely by brother Jacob. The Waldorf educational approach, with its emphasis on the arts, helped make the transition to homeschooling a smooth one. It would have been a much smoother transition, however, if not for legal problems that began almost immediately.

"A guy in a suit with a briefcase and dark sunglasses would come around and ring the doorbell," Aaron remembers. "We'd answer the door and he'd talk to Mom. Shortly after that, in 1981, we moved, up to the farm. We kids didn't really know why at the time, but I think it had to do with the social workers coming by and checking on us." After the move, the man with the dark sunglasses stopped visiting.

The problems the Timlins were experiencing as some of Michigan's earliest homeschoolers only slightly influenced their decision to move. Hugh had a lifelong dream of raising a family in a homesteading lifestyle—a dream Sandra shared. It was time to live that dream.

The farm home, "hardly finished," stood in northern Michigan's middle of nowhere. Indoor plumbing and electricity were among the missing, but there *were* lots of little mouths to feed "off the land." After the move, Hugh stopped going to work and instead focused his attention on the homestead. He labored on a sheep ranch off and on during the lambing and shearing seasons, and sometimes sold his own lambs to Detroit area food co-ops. "Once in a great while, he would land an art commission of some kind," Aaron says. "That night, we would have steak."

"My parents were pretty independent," he recalls. "Homeschooling just fit right in with all of this."

As a 10-year-old, Aaron accepted the decision to homeschool as a matter of fact, even though he didn't quite understand why he wasn't going to school anymore beyond what he picked up by overhearing his dad's "adult talk" or interviews with others. "Now that I share conversation about it with Dad, I can see it was just a thing my parents have about public schools," he says. "They didn't agree with the competition, the test system, the lack of attention when there's one teacher for 30 kids. They wanted us to learn what we wanted to learn on our own."

One day while visiting his grandparents, Aaron caught a brief TV news report on homeschooling. "There were three or four kids sitting down," he remembers. "The parent was at a chalkboard and the children raised their hands and did all those little school things. It was really strange because I didn't think that was what homeschooling was all about."

From Aaron's view, "Homeschooling was about more time to play in the sandbox, going off and learning to spin, learning to draw if you wanted to draw, learning to make jam or cook or hunt. And," he adds, "escaping to the back property if we had arithmetic problems to do. We'd run away and play as far away as we could and come back when it was too late." With two artists as parents and teachers, all of the Timlin children freely explored a variety of mediums and developed a broad potpourri of artistic talents.

Aaron's strongest interests lay in theater, writing, and acting. He watched the Academy Awards every year. Hearing the actors, directors, and producers speak about keeping your dream alive inspired him. They also kept Aaron, in his rural Michigan home, questioning silently and persistently, "How, how, how?"

The boy and his brothers and sisters enjoyed play with neighborhood friends. Winter weekends were filled with sledding, and summer was time to teach friends about horses. Festivals and parties were family affairs. Siblings were and still are best friends, including Rebekah, who today is listening to Aaron's interview from the art gallery where they both work. Aaron can't help himself; her presence begs comments like, "My sister spent all her time reading and never did chores or anything." Brother Daniel liked staying up all night. "If you woke up at 5 in the morning," Aaron says, "his kerosene lamp was still on. He was still drawing."

Farm chores and wandering all over the place came so naturally to Aaron that he didn't give his lifestyle a second thought, that is, until as an 11-year-old he started going to the Monday farm auction. Farmers always questioned why he wasn't in school. He explained homeschooling over and over again. "That's when I started to wonder about homeschooling and became a bit uncomfortable about it," says Aaron.

After the Fall

It was a chilly morning, so the boys (who slept on one side of the loft while the girls slept on the other) waited in their beds until the wood stove warmed up the house at least a little before they ventured downstairs. Aaron, Jacob, and Daniel decided it would be fun to get inside their *Star Wars* sleeping bags to look like ghosts, then give the girls a good scare.

Jacob started down the narrow hallway first. Before Aaron got very far, he heard a big *thump*. Cardboard cans filled with clothes lined the loft where a rail was yet to be installed and, unable to see, Jacob walked into them and fell to the floor below.

Jacob wasn't breathing. Hugh frantically administered CPR as the stunned family waited for help to arrive. "Rebekah and I took a Catholic statue my grandmother had given us. I didn't even know what it meant," Aaron remembers. "I just grabbed it to hold onto it, then ran to the outhouse where I cried and prayed he'd be okay."

An ambulance raced Jacob to the hospital, where he was whisked away by helicopter to another hospital. When Jacob regained consciousness, the medical personnel, as is customary, asked him a series of questions designed to determine if the blow to his head had affected his mental functions. When asked what school he attended, he stated he was homeschooling.

Once recovered, Jacob went home with his family, only to be visited that day by a Department of Social Services (DSS) worker routinely investigating possible child abuse. She told Hugh she was considering educational neglect charges. After a 2-hour visit with the family, she realized there was no need for charges.

It was almost a year later "when another DSS worker heard about us and brought a case of educational neglect to probate court," says Hugh who had, over the years, established a relationship with Clonlara School director Pat Montgomery. Pat and the director of DSS happened to be old friends. At Pat's request, the director investigated the situation, only to discover that the term "educational neglect" didn't exist in DSS policy.

"The director called a statewide meeting and informed all DSS workers they were not to pursue homeschoolers on charges of educational neglect," Hugh recalls. "That was a landmark moment for homeschoolers because the DSS had been the source of their greatest hassles. The worker who brought the case against us was ordered to drop the case, which he did, but probate court judges have the prerogative of continuing charges and our judge did just that."

When Hugh arrived at the courthouse for the pretrial hearing, the judge warned him that the day's proceedings could end with him losing custody of his children. "During the Vietnam War, I had refused induction, but I had *never* in my life experienced the kind of fear I felt that day," recalls Hugh.

As a low-income family, the Timlins retained a lawyer through Legal Aid. "I kind of had to educate him as to how much we would concede," Hugh continues. "Administering a California Achievement Test (CAT) to our three school-age children was about as far as I was prepared to go."

With enough new reading skills to take the test, Aaron scored at grade level. Jacob, intimidated by the procedure, never completed it. Rebekah, at age 9, scored around the twelfth grade level on all sections of the test. When the judge received the results, he dropped the charge. By then, the Timlins had spent a year in court and dealt with DSS for 5 years.

"I remember how drained my parents were during that time," says Aaron. "It didn't stop them from homeschooling, though. They weren't going to let anybody stop them from their life's voyage."

In the laid-back, child-centered atmosphere of the Timlin's homeschooling homestead, neither Aaron nor Jacob could think of a good reason to learn how to read, not when sister Rebekah enjoyed it so much, was good at it, and would read aloud to them often. As the courts continued intruding into the family's educational business, though, the pressure was on. Hugh and Sandra, however gently, were forced to transfer some of that pressure onto their children. The boys had best learn how to read.

> **The judge warned Hugh he could lose custody of his children. "During the Vietnam War, I had refused induction, but I had *never* in my life experienced the kind of fear I felt that day."**

Fortunately for the boys, the internal drive to master the skill had kicked in around this time, too (Aaron was 13 and Jacob 12). They wanted to read books Rebekah wasn't reading out loud. They started at the beginning, with Dick and Jane books. "I didn't necessarily enjoy them, trying to make sense of what the words meant and how they sounded," Aaron says. "The other thing we read was a really old series of little novels for children. Jacob and I would take them outside on a sunny, spring day and put the books on the backs of our pet sheep. I remember that so well," says Aaron, pausing as he thinks back, "that point of learning. The feel of the warm wool with the book laying on it, just lying there reading, chickens wobbling around us."

He also remembers his first homeschool book assignment. "Dad told me to read *Animal Farm*. That was the first book I read and said, 'Wow! I'm glad I learned how to read!' We'd always discuss what I was reading."

Until then, Aaron had always felt he was in charge of his education. When the big reading push came, though, "that's when I didn't have much control over what I was able to do," he says. "My parents weren't really strict, but they said, 'Okay, we need to read this many pages. So let's sit down and spend this many hours together and read.'"

Government High School

Despite the fact he found reading difficult at first, Aaron soon enjoyed it and remained largely content learning at home, that is, until curiosity about how other people learned got to him. He enjoyed summers with a friend who came to visit his grandfather down the road a piece. The friend's family eventually moved into the neighborhood as both boys reached high school age, and they enrolled in government school together.

"I about killed Aaron!" Hugh jokes. "But Sandra and I talked about it and accepted that the reason we homeschooled our children was to bring them to the point of making conscientious, mature, and free decisions. It was obvious to us that he wasn't doing it lightly and he had very good reasons that he explained to us. We really had no choice because we had succeeded in our goal. It was, I guess, the logical conclusion."

Hugh decided that if Aaron was making an informed decision to go to school, he himself would run for school board to be in a position to have something to say about the way the school was run. "It took 36 signatures to get my name on the ballot," says Hugh, "and I think that's as many votes as I got. People by this time were convinced that we were absolutely—"

"Nuts." I complete the sentence for him as we share a good laugh and the momentary meeting of the minds available to those who have survived similar experiences.

Aaron went off to government school, "but the electorate" decided against putting Hugh on the board.

"When I first went in there, the strangest thing to me was all the kids," Aaron says. "That's my first memory—just standing in the middle of the hall and all these kids running towards me. They weren't *really* running towards me; they were just going to their classes, but all those faces were crazy."

"I couldn't understand their tests, and bombed them. My first 2 years, I barely got by with C's and D's. The exception was English where I got A's my first semester, so they moved me into advanced English." Aaron continues, "A lot of the teachers there knew what we'd been doing since this was the school system that took us to court. When the advanced English teacher found out who I was, she didn't pay much attention to me. A certain group of kids sat on one side of the room and the other group sat on the other side. She focused most of her attention on the other group, the one I wasn't in. I realized there really were such things as teacher's pets. She actually sent me back to general English, which was fine with me because that teacher liked me a lot better and respected me. I just kept doing extra credit work there."

> **"This was the school system that took us to court. When the advanced English teacher found out who I was, she didn't pay much attention to me."**

"But she told all her other classes that I was homeschooled and doing great work, and here I was just trying to fit in and feeling like I didn't fit in at all. People worry about feeling isolated in homeschooling, but *this* was the first time I ever felt social isolation. When all the kids found out about homeschooling, they'd always ask, 'Wasn't it really hard?' It wasn't; I never saw it as hard."

Just as it often takes a couple of years to get the effects of schooling out of a child come home to learn, it took Aaron equally long to assimilate into the school program. "By junior year, I started to learn how to take a test and how to study," he explains. "That's when I really understood what Dad meant when he said the public school system is only designed for one-third of its students. The other two-thirds either drop out or just barely make it by. My brother and I were part of that two-thirds," he states matter-of-factly. "I learned the system and learned how to succeed in it. My brother barely made it the whole way through. Rebekah was one of that one-third it was designed for and she could totally understand that way of learning. She was secretary of her freshman class and president by her senior year."

By Aaron's senior year, he finally felt he had found his place in the school. "It was with *any* clique," he says. "I was comfortable with myself, so I pretty much became friends with everybody, which probably came from my upbringing not categorizing people."

Finding Work That Fits

Aaron took one job with his friend while in high school. A ski lodge paid them 2 dollars an hour to make sure the ropes that pull people to the top of the hill didn't get off track. When they did, Aaron had to go up the hill on a snowmobile to fix it. "I got two paychecks from there and I quit," he says. "I couldn't stand being that cold."

Following high school graduation, Aaron took a trip to Germany with Youth for Understanding, a nonprofit educational organization that provides young people around the world opportunities to live with host families in other cultures. Upon returning to the States, Aaron left his small town and moved to Detroit. Here he spent a lot of time volunteering, for the Detroit Institute of Art, the Artists' Market, and the Michigan Kidney and Pulmonary Disease Camp for children. He supported himself by working with kidney, AIDS, and HIV patients in a hospital dialysis unit. The work was intense, but Aaron noticed how easily he could talk with older patients whose backgrounds included living with outhouses rather than indoor plumbing and learning at home. "I could often relate more to them than to contemporaries who talked about TV programs and told jokes about them I'll never understand."

> "Homeschooling gave me the opportunity to realize what it was I even wanted to do or be."

Courting his first girlfriend, Aaron found it strange that her parents got nervous that he wasn't thinking about college or mapping out the rest of his life. That was at least part of the reason he wanted to enroll in Wayne State University's nursing program. The university was reluctant because Aaron's grades had been so bad during his first 2 years of high school. "A friend of my dad's knew the dean of the nursing department and got me in," Aaron explains, "so it wasn't *what* I knew, it was *who* I knew at that time, like it almost always is."

Aaron realizes there is a difference between his educational experience and that of others who spend 13 or more years getting funneled through a school system only to wind up when they're finished not knowing what they want out of life. "Homeschooling gave me the opportunity to realize what it was I even wanted to do or be. I think most people are just put into a category, or their parent or school sees they're talented in one area and says, 'Oh, that's what you should be, a doctor,' when really all they want to do is draw. They have that whole fear related to success that my brothers and sisters and I never had instilled in us. I think time to yourself has a great deal to do with it—time to listen to what's going on inside yourself."

It took 2 years in the nursing program for Aaron to listen to what was going on inside himself. He realized he wasn't in the program because he thought he would be a good nurse. Instead, he was trying to do what he thought others, especially his girlfriend's parents, wanted him to do. Once he saw that, he left the program.

He continued to work at the hospital, but deep inside he knew that he "wanted to make a difference in the world that went beyond the basement of a large corporate monster hospital." Aaron worked hard and saved harder. Three years ago, he bought a "decrepit yellow storefront flanked by empty lots on Rosa Parks Boulevard in Detroit's Woodbridge neighborhood," or so a January 29, 1999 *Detroit Free Press* article described the location. Aaron agrees with the assessment. "Water pipes were broken, the roof was falling in, and the walls and ceilings were collapsing," he says. "When I walked into that building, though, I saw beyond the disrepair to large loft apartments, a restaurant, an art gallery. I just knew it would be home to something great."

As Aaron and Rebekah toured the newly purchased building during one of her visits, she came up with an idea befitting the Timlin family. Why not create a family art show to raise money to pay the taxes on the farm (which is now an artists' retreat), and help pay her expenses as a student at the University of Glasgow in Scotland? The result of that first show—which did cover the farm's taxes for a year—was the birth of the Detroit Contemporary, one of the city's "most unusual" and "way hip" art galleries, which Aaron owns and directs.

Aaron believes his homeschooling experience gave him a more creative approach to problem solving than most people develop. He manages an apartment building "so they give me a free place to live," and recently took on the paying role of curator of an artists' Web site, GyroDesign. He'd like to expand the gallery into a museum. "I can see solutions to some of the problems with the city's kids," he states with conviction. "I'm going to start an arts education program here, and I think that comes from my upbringing and my homeschooling. The public schools aren't worth anything, so if we give some of those kids some direction it could have a positive impact on society."

An arts education program takes funding—lots of it—but Aaron has an idea for this, too. "In May, I'm going to paint a refrigerator box all black and paint in white lettering on all the sides, 'Got Art?'—a play on the milk campaign. Then," he says with building enthusiasm, "I'll walk the 645 miles from Detroit to New York and take pledges for this program that will team up kids with artists, a mentoring program. I've already got the possibility of starting in the Detroit Institute of Arts, ending up at the Frick Collection in New York, and meeting Sam Saks who directs that collection."

With the gallery's success and all the plans, you wouldn't think Aaron would contemplate different work. But the little boy inside still remembers watching the Oscar presentations on TV and may have discovered the answer to the question that never went away: How do I keep the dream alive? The gallery just may be the vehicle for not only keeping alive the dream of writing screenplays and acting, but also fulfilling it. "Through the gallery, I've been networking with local independent filmmakers and others involved in various aspects of the arts. I'm getting closer to understanding how the whole process works. We've had a few film shows here, so strangely enough everything is coming into place."

Unmarried, Aaron believes one day he'll homeschool his own children, but he'll leave the city and its culture he loves to do it. "Eventually, I'll either move to a farm or move to Ireland and live off the land, similar to what my parents did. I'll educate my children in how to live with the earth." This future homeschooling dad knows he learned his parents' values by living intimately with them on the farm.

Today, Hugh and Sandra live apart. Hugh teaches part time at Wayne State University and has a major art exhibition opening. Sandra, who changed her surname to Two Moons after the divorce when the name was presented to her in a dream from an Indian messenger, splits her time between Canada and New Mexico, where she built a solar home from straw and fieldstone. Five years ago, she became a naturopathic doctor.

> **"Both of my parents left with me and continue to nurture much wisdom for the body and the mind," says Aaron.**

"Both of my parents left with me and continue to nurture much wisdom for the body and the mind," he says. "I call my father when I'm struggling with a relationship or with ideas for the gallery or my own artwork. I call my mother when I have questions about health or when I want to escape the humdrum of the city and remember the beauty of a secluded life."

The wisdom of pursuing dreams recently revealed itself to Aaron in the form of a young boy who visited the gallery with a group of children from the neighborhood directly behind the gallery, a neighborhood the locals refer to as "ghost town."

"I was frantically preparing for the opening of a major exhibition," says Aaron. "I invited them to check out the work of over 100 local artists, and they toured the four exhibition rooms. As they left, some of the kids commented on the weirdness of the art."

One little boy, however, said to Aaron, "This is a great dream."

Startled, Aaron simply replied, "Thank you."

"This *is* a dream, isn't it?" the boy asked.

"Yes, I guess it is," Aaron answered.

"I thought so," said the boy. "Is it yours?"

When Aaron said yes, the boy told him with a smile, "You have a great dream."

IT'S A CRIME *to keep a kid from being able to reach his potential. Just because a kid is home-schooled, he can't compete for a scholarship, go to college, and maybe get a one-in-a-million chance to make it to a professional level and fulfill a dream? Just because some guy sitting behind a desk somewhere doesn't want him to be able to play? Really, it's a crime.*

5

Coming Home to the Champion Within

JASON TAYLOR

Born: September 1, 1974; Pittsburgh, Pennsylvania
Homeschooling: 1989–1992
Family: Parents—Anthony and Georgia; Siblings—Tiffanie (27), Joy (13), Grace (11), Noah (10)
Most memorable wisdom about life or learning: If you believe it, you can achieve it.
Favorite study: Early years—playing basketball; Middle years—same; Teen years—same and playing football
Current work: NFL Miami Dolphins defensive end—#99 (since 1997)

According to all reports, Jason Taylor is the first homeschooler to play in the National Football League. As a result of the Taylor family's decision to homeschool, Jason's journey to a starting position as defensive end for the Miami Dolphins was filled with challenges. Had it not been for homeschooling, though, the journey might never have happened at all.

Homeschooling:
The Experiment

Jason attended government schools in Pittsburgh, Pennsylvania, through third grade, at which time the family opted for private school. They even bought an old house right behind the school "so we could be right there," Georgia says. Despite the fact that her children were always late for school because they lived so close, Mom was happy with the choice. The school was big enough to offer good teachers and programs and small enough that individual children didn't get lost.

Georgia first learned about home education from Renee, a homeschooling church friend. "I don't know if I'd want to do that," was Georgia's response.

"Why?" asked Renee.

Georgia answered, "I don't know if I could."

"Oh, yes you can!" said Renee. "Everybody can do this." Renee explained to Georgia how Pennsylvania law had changed, and homeschooling parents were no longer required to be certified teachers. A parental high-school diploma was now all that was legally necessary.

Like many before her, Georgia began wondering if homeschooling would work for her preschool-age children. She considered homeschooling her older children Jason and Tiffanie as an experiment; Tiffanie, a gifted and talented pupil, could finish a light load of requirements at home as a senior, and Jason could always go back to school if it didn't work. While homeschooling could be an intentional act, it didn't need to be an "eternal act," says Georgia. "We *wanted* it to be, but we didn't know anything about it yet."

Why would a parent take a risk like this when a reputedly good private school sat next door?

"We knew even the private school system had control over our children's education," explains Georgia. "We wanted to be the ones to decide what our children learned. We teach them that this is wrong and this is right, and we didn't want anyone teaching them differently. When that happens," she continues, "the parents' integrity is destroyed. The children no longer feel the parents know what they're talking about."

> "We wanted to be the ones to decide what our children learned."

Renee planted the seed of homeschooling in Georgia's mind in early spring. Georgia sent away for information from the sources Renee supplied and decided she wanted the structure of Christian Liberty Academy's complete curriculum. By June, she had ordered homeschooling materials and enrolled Jason and Tiffanie in the program that keeps students' records. The Taylors were ready for the educational experiment.

Georgia remembers her family looking at each other after a couple of days of homeschooling and wondering, "Is this what home-schooling's like? Are we doing it right?" She laughs out loud at the memory.

Tiffanie began to realize that all the "prep time" that went into getting ready for school had been wasted time. Jason saw that book-work proceeded a lot more quickly at home. "At home you don't have all the interruptions of recess, having to walk to your next class, teachers correcting people, and people goofing off in the back." And, he adds, "You don't have to worry about school shootings, either."

Jason recalls wanting to remain at school with his buddies. "Home-schooling was my parents' idea," he says. "We were living under their roof and that's what they wanted to do, so I had to try it." He had been a decent school student but, he adds, was "a typical teenage guy who had a lot of other things I wanted to do besides schoolwork. I wasn't bringing home F's, but I wasn't bringing home A+'s, either."

The following year, instead of purchasing an entire curriculum, Jason and Georgia chose some courses from their previous curriculum provider and supplemented them with bookstore purchases of workbooks, vocabulary books, and "a lot of economics."

> **One day, at the age of 13, Jason was standing on a street corner alone when a man accosted him with a gun.**

Even though a nearby support group offered classes to homeschoolers every Friday, at that point the Taylors had neither the time nor a need to participate. "I started homeschooling in 1989. I had babies in '87, '88, and '89," Georgia explains. "Tiffany had already graduated and was planning on getting married. Jason was busy constantly with football and basketball, so we were *never* here. Those were years of football season games, basketball season games, then springtime was here, and I had one of my babies in June and another year in August. Life was full!" Georgia laughs.

Jason had played power forward and center on a basketball team since junior high and harbored hopes of earning a college scholarship through the game. "If I didn't get a scholarship," he says, "there wasn't going to be a real good chance that I could go to college because my parents didn't have the money for it."

Homeschooling days often began for Jason at 6 A.M. when "I'd go down to the courts and work out for a while," he says. Indeed, dad Anthony frequently recalls seeing Jason at the basketball court, scraping off snow so he could practice while the other kids his age were riding off to school on a bus.

"I'd shoot around and come back at 8 A.M. to start my schoolwork. It was self-paced, so I'd work through it, and Mom and my super-brilliant sister were always there to help me, too," says Jason. After lunch it was back to the playground for basketball or off to karate lessons. Later, it was either basketball or football practice or games, depending on the season. Somehow Jason also managed to work for a disaster restoration company from the time he was 16 until he went to college.

Volunteer Experiences Full of Life Lessons

The younger members of the Taylor family are still growing up and homeschooling in one of the many residential neighborhoods that constitute greater Pittsburgh. Dad Anthony works as a corrections officer and supervisor. Mom Georgia, a computer science degree holder who once worked for the U.S. Department of Defense doing "some things" she can't discuss, stays home with the children. Jason's older sister, Tiffanie, lives on the same street with husband Sam and their four daughters.

The Taylors are active church members, and Jason grew up donating much of his time to church activities. As a pre-teen he was part of a puppet team that visited Pittsburgh's Children's Hospital monthly to entertain the kids. As he grew, he joined a group of teens that visited nursing homes to sing for the residents. These were Jason's "tame" volunteer experiences.

He often joined a group of men who went into the worst areas of Pittsburgh to set up coffee and doughnut time in the winter or to hand out collected clothing to those who needed it. One day, at the age of 13, he was standing on a street corner alone when a man accosted him with a gun. A fellow church member, who was nearby and had kept an eye on Jason, stepped in between the two and convinced the gun-toter to put it away.

A multi-church sponsored group of teens were sent on a 2-week mission to Grenada to help rebuild after the war. Fourteen-year-old Jason was looking forward to performing construction work (which he still loves). His entry into the island country was a bit rough, however. He misplaced his birth certificate and was held back by the custom guards for an hour until his group finally convinced them to let him through.

In Grenada, he passed out candy he had brought for the children. "They hid it to treasure it," Jason says. "They didn't even eat it." This was hard for him to understand, especially when he was trying to survive on the same meals as the children, the "brown stuff that would run across my plate," he says. Days were tiring but fulfilling as Jason labored with a construction crew. In the evenings after work, the teens performed song-and-dance programs for the children or handed out clothing to those in need. Jason made many friends, including the daughter of an ambassador to Grenada.

While visiting the market one afternoon, Jason took a picture of a native only to have the angry islander come after him with a machete. The man's belief system led him to accept that Jason had just captured his soul. Jason took to his heels with the man running strong behind him. A good runner himself, Jason zigzagged through the market until he finally lost the native in the fish market. He jumped on to a packed bus to return to his residence, anxiously looked out the window, and there was the angry man leering at him. Wondering what else might happen to him while in Grenada, the frightened teen bought himself a machete. Today that machete hangs in the Taylors' kitchen, a constant reminder of a faraway place where people are not as fortunate as they are.

Soon it was time to go home, and the group set off to the airport. They got as far as the one red light in the middle of town where traffic and confusion blocked their way. They learned that Jason's friend's father, the ambassador, had just been assassinated there.

"Happening at that time in his life, I think those things sobered him a little bit," says Georgia of the experiences. "I'm sure they will always stay with him."

Why Aren't You on My Football Team?

A recent accounting reveals that 23 states allow children educated at home to play interscholastic sports, that is, if you include Vermont, which allows inclusion on individual, but not team sports. Pennsylvania was on that growing list when Jason was homeschooling. One day, Jason was working on his car outside the house when the Woodland Hills High School football coach drove by. The coach stopped and asked the 6' 5" tall, 240-pound Jason, "Why aren't you on my football team?"

Jason answered, "I always play basketball. I've played street football, but never organized football." ("I think I actually told him I'm a heck of a street ball player," he adds.)

"There are try-outs in a couple of days," the coach informed him. "Let me know if you need a way to get there, and I'll come pick you up."

When Jason asked Georgia if he could try it, she answered, "Go for it."

Unfortunately, the Woodland Hills High School board officials weren't quite as supportive. They said no. According to a *USA Today* article by Carolyn White, it took some advocacy from the football coaches to convince the board to reverse their decision. In the meantime, Jason missed a couple of

> Jason was working on his car outside the house when the Woodland Hills High School football coach drove by. The coach stopped and asked, "Why aren't you on my football team?"

games and had to constantly remind himself, "I didn't do anything wrong."

Jason made the junior varsity team as a tight end and free safety but didn't play very much during his first year. After he worked his way up to the varsity team, he played a very good senior year of football, observed by an Akron University scout. Jason earned a diploma from Christian Liberty Academy, took the SAT (Scholastic Assessment Test) and the ACT (American College Test), and racked up scores high enough to exceed National Collegiate Athletic Association (NCAA) scholarship requirements. Akron University, with an NCAA Division 1 team and located just 2 short hours from Pittsburgh, offered Jason a full scholarship to come play for them.

Settled into the university and attending classes, Jason faithfully practiced for 5 hours every day with Akron University's Zips. As a freshman, he was tagged for a starting position as a linebacker. Two days before the first game, on his eighteenth birthday, the NCAA declared Jason's scholarship invalid, refusing "to honor [his] test scores and saying he hadn't met core course requirements," according to *USA Today*. Mom and Dad quickly responded, threatening court action before the NCAA also reversed its decision after almost a month of legal wrangling.

"I think the NCAA had problems because homeschooling was new to them at the time, and they didn't have any rules for it," says Georgia. "They didn't know how to 'classify' homeschooling. The delay with the NCAA in taking care of the problem caused Jason to miss 3 weeks of practice and team activities." The athletic association finally returned Jason's scholarship, but not before he was "red-shirted," meaning he had to sit out an entire year of football. Athletes are granted 5 years in which to complete 4 years of play. Jason had just used up his "reserve" year.

At the university, Jason majored in political science and criminal justice. The double major even made the dean's list a few times while becoming a shining star on the college football field—and playing basketball.

In his senior year, Jason became a defensive end. It's the football position he would take when, in the third round of the 1997 draft, the Miami Dolphins chose him to don the #99 jersey. At the beginning of his first season, the Dolphins moved the rookie into a starting position.

> **At the beginning of his first season, the Dolphins moved the rookie into a starting position.**

In December of 1998, Jason broke his collarbone and was out for the rest of that season. Injuries were nothing new to Jason. "Every finger on his body's been broken, he has a plate and nine screws in his right arm to protect it, and he's played in the pros with a broken forearm," reports Georgia.

The Dolphins are hanging on to Jason into yet another season, likely because they know what kind of player they have in the homeschooled young man. "My son has always been a concentrated individual," says Georgia. "Even if they're losing—you watch those games—he plays like only he's going to save the day, like Mighty Mouse."

You Never Understand the System Until You Get Out of It

When Georgia visited Jason after his move to the Dolphin's home base in Florida for his new job as football player, she was shocked to see how he was living. "Here he was a millionaire, and all he had were his sheet and blanket from college and a bed because he knew he had to have a place to rest." Mother and son went shopping, and today Jason is more comfortably settled. He is unmarried, although Katina, a sister of a teammate, currently occupies quite a bit of his time. A public school graduate herself, Jason's girl-friend finds homeschooling intriguing.

Jason would like to marry one day and raise a family. He's not sure about homeschooling for his children but admits, "It will be different when I actually *have* children." He recalls that he wasn't initially thrilled with the idea of homeschooling and says, "Looking back now, there's nothing I would criticize about it at all. It's led me to where I wanted to go, so there couldn't be anything wrong with it."

> **"We learned you can help anyone become a champion. It's just a matter of finding out what that champion is champ of."**

Georgia gives homeschooling credit for Jason's success. "When we freed up his schedule by homeschooling him, we freed him to be educated in what he was good at," she explains. "We never knew what was in Jason, what his abilities were. Not until he was homeschooled were we able to see what we needed to do as parents to support the abilities he was capable of excelling in. We learned you can help anyone become a champion. It's just a matter of finding out what that champion is champ of."

"I heard someone say this once, but I'd never realized it—you never understand the system you're in until you get out of it. That's when you can stand back to examine it. Our children went to a very good school. It wasn't until they were out that I could see the unnecessary time spent. I could see money wasn't being allocated right. I could see the children weren't being offered things they could have been if only somebody took the time to do it and be concerned about it."

Like so many other homeschoolers, Jason carried with him into adulthood a simple, but important message. "I know I can look into something I'm interested in and learn it," he says, "whether it's by reading books or finding it on TV or talking to the right person. I know I can do it myself."

When asked if he thinks other teens could homeschool, even if mom and dad work, Jason says, "I think they certainly can. Again it puts the pressure on the kid to get up and do his work. He's not going to have Miss Smith shoving it down his throat every day. You've got to get up and do it. If you fail, there's only person you can point a finger at."

I ask if that's what makes it fun and meaningful, when your education becomes your responsibility. "Yeah!" Jason answers with the most enthusiasm expressed during the interview. "And I think it helped me when I went to college. If you don't show up for class in college, no one's going to call you or come get you to take you to class. Homeschooling prepares you for that, also. You get a syllabus and a book; it's up to you to get your butt to class and learn."

Jason was just 23 years old when fulfillment of his dreams thrust him into responsibility for more money and fame than many people see in a lifetime. "Once you get into it there are a lot of pressures," he says. "The homeschooling has helped me be accountable for my actions and handle the pressure to get things done. That has carried over. Handling the notoriety isn't something you learn in books, I'll tell you that much. The scrutiny is one of the toughest things outside of the pressure to perform every week, to do my job, and push to be the best at what I do. You have the Monday morning quarterbacks that want to criticize everything you do and the media pressures and pressure from the fans. There's a lot that goes into it, but it's a great job if you can keep your head on straight."

> "Handling the notoriety isn't something you learn in books, I'll tell you that much."

Success is measured differently for all of us, Jason believes. "There are people that can't do some of the things I can do, and I can't do some of the things they can do," he explains. "When someone makes the most out of the situation he's in, I think that's when he's successful."

"My situation is different," Jason continues. "There are a lot of things I want to do in life. I don't think at 25 I or anyone else can say we're successful. Hopefully at the end I can look *back* and say I was. One of the sayings I have on the wall in my office is: Success is a constant journey, not a destination."

When I ask Jason about future plans, he replies, "It's funny that you ask that. I was just talking with Katina about how much is going on right now in the NFL [National Football League]. A lot of the players are getting into trouble; now they're going to jail for murder. Derrick Thomas, a player for the Kansas City Chiefs, died, and Tom Landry, a great coach, passed away yesterday. I was explaining to her about how you can sit there and plan and hope that you're going to get to a certain level, but you never know if you'll get a chance to do it. I take it a day at a time," he concludes. "I've got a lot of things I want to do in the future, but you're never promised tomorrow."

Despite that philosophical attitude, Jason does have a "perfect plan" in mind. "That would be to play football for about 10 or 12 years, make a ton of money, take care of my mother, take care of my sister, and not have to do much of anything besides what I want to do when retired. It would be nice if football could eventually get me into other ventures, with TV and the like."

After speaking with Jason, I have little doubt that he will "keep his head on straight." Does this mean he'll continue to regard playing with the Miami Dolphins as a great job? I hope so. I like to think more homeschoolers will be rooting for my favorite football team when the leaves start falling again.

THERE'S NO WAY *I could have learned as much about business at such an early age in a typical structured school environment. Home-schooling's flexibility helped me an awful lot.*

6

The Multimillion Dollar Man

AARON FESSLER

Born: October 5, 1972; New Carlisle, Ohio
Homeschooling: 1982–1990
Family: Parents—Robert and Diana; Siblings—Angel (30), Anne Marie (25), Andrew (22), Elizabeth (18), Olivia (15)
Most memorable wisdom about life or learning: Work has its rewards—and if you enjoy what you do it really isn't work.
Favorite study: Early years—electronics, computers, and music; Middle years—piano; Teen years—computers; entire area of business from a fairly early age
Work: Since 1995, owner of Allegro (sold 6 weeks prior to interview for $55 million)

For some families, the decision to homeschool is based on a belief that God commands deep involvement in the children's education. So it was for Robert and Diana Fessler and their six children in1982; the couple had had a profound religious experience the previous spring that led them to reconsider their approach to education.

Aaron remembers his brief stint in public school punctuated by "F's for effort and A's for grades. I rarely did my homework and got paddled by the principal. When I did do my work, it was fine. I just really didn't put my heart and soul into school because it was difficult to operate in an environment with the broad skill ranges of 30 kids. I didn't find it particularly challenging and I didn't seem to connect with a lot of the kids at school. I was one of the skinny guys who got chased around and sat on a lot."

In their rural home in New Carlisle, Ohio, the Fesslers had neighbors who were also large homeschooling families—an unusual situation in 1982. Even still, Aaron explains, "There was often a real element of fear and concern. Homeschooling wasn't anything you flouted or told anyone about, so it was a real principled type of approach." A measure of discretion was sometimes neccesary in the days when homeschooling either stood on precarious legal ground or was downright illegal.

Healthy Homeschooling Days

The Fessler's approach included daily schedules that Diana drew up a couple of weeks at a time. "We were all at home at the same time," says Aaron. "It was usually somewhat of a requirement, especially in the morning hours, that all the kids be present in the same room." The family soon noticed another of homeschooling's often hidden benefits for younger siblings: Even when the little ones appear not to be paying attention, they pick up lots of the information flying around them. Aaron vividly remembers a sister, still too young to speak in legible sentences, treating the family to her interpretation of Bible verses.

The family's lifestyle provided lots of opportunity for exercise, contributing to good health for all. When the day's routine includes caring for animals, chopping and hauling wood, and tending a garden, coupled with acreage and a creek to explore, children spend lots of time out in the fresh air.

Throughout their homeschooling experience, the large family visited local nursing homes to perform favorite old songs and play games each month. Political campaigns became a favorite pastime, as was involvement in the growing homeschooling movement. Since all the homeschooling neighbors knew each other well, the children were playmates. Robert and Diana were careful about how much contact their children had with same-aged peers. They were concerned about negative external influences that could undermine their efforts to shape their children's characters.

> The family noticed another of homeschooling's often hidden benefits: Even when the little ones appear not to be paying attention, they pick up lots of information.

"That was a big area of concern to them so we really didn't have a lot of uncontrolled exposure to kids our age," says Aaron. Though the Fesslers chose not to involve their children in Sunday School or extracurricular activities like sports, Aaron never felt socially isolated. "My personal interests consumed all my excess energy," he explains. "One of the important skills of being a mature and socialized adult is to interact with people outside your peer grouping and age range. When you're homeschooled, certainly you're exposed to younger kids and older kids and adults all at the same time." And, of course, there were all those siblings and homeschooled neighbors.

When Aaron was still a toddler, Robert started his own business, Dayton Sign Rental, and provided a good, early entrepreneurial role model for his children. Aaron and Andrew worked with Robert in the afternoons and on Saturdays, helping to erect signs and making necessary repairs. Riding to and from work together afforded the trio many opportunities for in-depth discussions.

At the same time, Robert was providing something else of equal importance. "I know Dad made a number of career choices in an effort to be more involved with homeschooling," Aaron says. "He relocated his business to be closer to family life. He came home in the middle of the day and dealt with situations and helped with our education. I know he could have pushed more aggressively for more financial rewards or career fulfillment, whatever that might be, but family is very, very important to him and he made that a tangible reality in our lives."

Within the principled homeschooling approach, all the Fessler children were encouraged to make their interests known, and their parents did their best to help those seeds grow. Most of the academics were completed in the morning, freeing the entire afternoon for Aaron to focus on the music, business, and technology pursuits he enjoyed. Aaron's interest in business began to flourish with a paper route at the age of 13.

An Entrepreneur Is Born

"One of my most distinct memories of that was the realization that on the weekly route I made 5 cents for every paper delivered. Frankly, it was an awful lot of work for that money," Aaron recalls. "However, I made 25 cents for each Sunday paper delivered. I can recall getting up at 3:30 or 4:00 on Sunday mornings and running through Huber Heights counting off 25 cents, 50 cents, as I dropped off the papers at front doors."

When the paper route ended, a business adventure centered on homeschooling began for Aaron. In 1989, Diana joined the Ohio Department of Education committee charged with rewriting the state's homeschooling regulations. When the regulations were made public, "there was no small amount of confusion among the general home-schooling population about how they should be implemented in terms of testing, notifying your superintendent, and other things," according to Aaron.

To help alleviate the confusion, Diana wrote a small booklet explaining the new regulations. Ever the entrepreneur, Aaron convinced his mom to let him front the money for printing and to make the booklet a business project during the homeschooling convention in Columbus the following weekend. He sold the booklets, which he had printed for about a dollar per copy, for 3 dollars each. He left the convention saying, "Wow, there's a real need out here!"

Suddenly, the entrepreneur was in full bloom. He convinced his mother to expand the booklet, which turned into a 100-page, typeset book titled *The Home Education Answers from Ohio Parents*. "Probably one of the most unbelievably niched products ever produced," he says with a laugh. Aaron convinced a local printer to help finance the project and produce several thousand copies. The project led to a small family mail-order business, run from a home office from the time he was 13 to 17 years old. One product does not a mail-order business make, so Aaron gathered other products of interest to homeschoolers—books, puzzles, and games—and created a catalog. The family also traveled to small homeschooling conventions when possible, and sold the materials from the back of their truck.

> **When the paper route ended, a business adventure centered on homeschooling began for Aaron.**

Running a mail-order business began consuming many of Aaron's afternoon hours. Education traditionalists might worry that his nose wasn't in a textbook but, as Aaron explains, "I learned a lot of skills at an early age; how to balance a checkbook, how to negotiate with vendors, how to look at cash flow, how to market and sell, how to administer a list of customers, how to deal with returns, and a whole host of different issues you don't typically learn at that age."

Aaron watched sales climb from $900 the first year to $3,000 the second, $12,000 the third, and $35,000 the next. The youth thought, "This is the best thing ever!"

As time passed, however, he realizes he learned two important lessons. "I discovered the hard way what profit margin means. What that means is that you hope to have more money left over than what you started with for all your work. After we closed out the books that last year, we had sold about 30,000 books, and our profit margin was *maybe* 5 to 10%. We had cleared $1,500 for a year's work—hard work—and a lot of risk."

He checked out a few colleges, then worked with computers for 8 months. Again, Aaron analyzed the work in terms of supporting a family some day and found it lacking.

The second lesson was to look at those who have been involved in the same industry for 4 to 5 years longer than you have been. Aaron's view was that, barring unusual circumstances, this would indicate where he could expect his business to be in the same amount of time. "When I looked at individuals who had been marketing to homeschoolers, I found that I'd have to sell an awful lot to support a standard of living that would exceed what I could do working at Taco Bell," says Aaron. "That helped guide me away from that and into another direction."

At the time, however, Aaron had no idea what that direction was. He checked out a few colleges that didn't quite capture his imagination, then worked with computers for a Christian organization in Chicago for 8 months. Again, Aaron analyzed the work in terms of supporting a family some day and found it lacking. When big sister, Angel, took off to Washington, D.C., for a job interview with the Home School Legal Defense Assocation (HSLDA), Aaron tagged along. "When the office manager saw me, he said, 'You look like a fine young strapping boy. We need somebody to put paper in the copy machines. Why don't you interview for the job since you're already here?'"

Aaron was 17 years old, and not the least bit interested in the legal or political issues of the HSLDA, but his family convinced him to take the job. In retrospect, he's grateful because the job led him to work on setting up the HSLDA computer system. At the time, they also wanted to connect their electronic messaging system to the Internet, so it fell to Aaron to figure out how to do this. His first solution was far too expensive. "It was then I realized there had to be an awful lot of other companies in a similar situation," Aaron recalls.

The problem, as he explains it, was that HSLDA used a proprietary network based mail system, designed to work within a company allowing employees to send electronic messages back and forth. At that time, that type of system generally wasn't designed to be connected directly to the Internet. The then 22-year-old Aaron quit his job and returned home to New Carlisle, never having seen the Internet. With a marker board, he set out to create what he perceived to be a more financially appropriate solution.

Aaron knew the $30,000–50,000 investment in hardware, followed by similarly steep investments in recurring service fees each year, was too great a price for the return for most businesses. But what if a brand new business bought the necessary hardware, then spread out the cost of the expensive assets by making its money charging monthly service fees to companies who wanted to use it?

Quickly, Aaron conducted a market study, saw enough interest, and decided to go for it. He had $5,000 and a couple of credit cards for the initial investment, and he was able to convince both Angel and Andrew to jump on board as employees. When Aaron talked to his folks about his plan, they said, "Aaron, we're not really sure what you're proposing here, but we'd love to have you back home. You're welcome to move up in the attic in the barn and we'll feed you dinner and do your laundry." In April 1995, a new company, Allegro, was born, just prior to two other companies who had come up with the same solution but hadn't yet gotten their products to market because they were focused on other services.

The young entrepreneur figured Allegro could last 5 months with his cash on hand, so he had to attract customers quickly. Aaron remembered his early homeschooling days and the collections part of delivering papers. "I had learned a lot about people skills and how to phrase things," he says. "Everything carried through." With the able help of his siblings, he made phone calls to magazines to find out names and addresses of potential customers. Each received a marketing letter and an order form in an envelope sporting a banner that asked, "Would you like to connect your mail to the Internet?"

"Considering how amateur the whole project was," Aaron remembers, "we were pretty shocked by how many responded. I figured we needed ten customers to break even." The Fessler siblings had those customers within 3 weeks. By the end of that year, there were 100 customers, and now they provide services to about 1,000. The increasing cash flow was always invested into more hardware, marketing, and appearances at trade shows.

> Within 8 months, the Fessler siblings ran out of room as well as phone lines in the barn. Two moves have brought Allegro to its current location—more than 10,000 square feet.

Within 8 months, the Fessler siblings ran out of room as well as phone lines in the barn. Two moves have brought Allegro to its current location in Dayton, Ohio—more than 10,000 square feet occupied by a couple of dozen employees.

Fessler sibling Anne Marie also hopped aboard Allegro's technical support team, even as well-meaning friends privately warned Aaron that, most often, sibling relationships suffer and crumble when they work together. "I'm happy to say the relationship with my siblings is just as strong as it's ever been," notes Aaron, "and they're a real joy to work with. They are very competent in their positions, unlike the situation in other companies where other employees might be truly better qualified for the positions."

Maybe, just maybe, the Fessler siblings are succeeding together—happily—because of the knowledge of each other they gained through years of learning at home together. Maybe it's because, as individuals, they maintain their own identity and dreams. Aaron admits he "kind of pushed them into Allegro." He appreciates Angel's warm disposition and versatility, and encourages Anne Marie in her interest in medicine. "I hope they all look at this business not as a destination but as a stepping stone to get to where they believe they want to be," says Aaron. "I think a worst possible scenario is where they end up retiring working for their older brother. That would be a tragedy. All of them have different dreams and desires and are working to achieve those, as well."

It is unlikely that any of the Fesslers will allow their dreams to fall by the wayside. "The homeschooling experience in self-sufficiency kicked in quite well," says Aaron. "Discipline was a pretty big part of our regimen growing up. Work ethic and work value systems were important."

In 1997, *Computer World Magazine* voted Allegro among the "Top 100 Emerging Technology Companies." At the close of 1999, Mail.com bought Allegro for $55 million.

Family First

Life is not all business and no play for Aaron. Piano lessons begun at age 9 and faithfully continued for a decade today provide him personal enjoyment in accompanying a small brass orchestra at church. Then there's time with 6½-month-old Jared, Aaron's first child with his wife, Kimber.

While Aaron believes homeschooling interfered with his meeting a quantity of members of the opposite sex, he concludes that's not a bad thing at the time of "hormone rages." He admits he quietly worried that any young lady he might meet would think him "a wacko guy."

So it was as young Aaron stood behind Kimber in the buffet line at a wedding reception "trying to think up some lame conversation." He asked her where she lived and discovered she had grown up and still lived in an environment similar to his own rural roots. Next, he asked where she had gone to school. "She said she'd been taught at home," Aaron remembers well. "I could just see right there this was going to happen."

Right now, it's likely that young Jared—as well as any subsequent children—will become second-generation homeschoolers. "That's something we'll have to discuss as we get closer to the time," Aaron says, "but it's something both of us feel pretty strongly about."

> Aaron remembers assuming as a young man "that when you reach some point, what it is you're supposed to do will just magically appear to you. I'm afraid I still haven't reached that point."

Aaron credits homeschooling in a large family for the self-motivation he possesses today. "Maybe in a smaller family it's different, but in a larger family there's only so much one person can do so there exists some burden on the part of the children to actually execute the plan that's laid out in from them. I think sometimes we read studies and find a good correlation between kids who've been homeschooled and their ability to do well in less structured but just as rigorous study environments, like a typical college. This skill set seems to be pretty prevalent among kids that have been taught at home because they've developed it at an earlier age, and it carries over even beyond formal schooling. The earlier you develop that skill set the better off you are."

Today, Mom Diana is serving a second term on the Ohio Sate Board of Education. Despite the sale of Allegro, Aaron, Angel, Anne Marie, and Andrew are still working with the company, in part because the buy-out created an economic incentive to do so. At such tender ages, retirement isn't even a consideration.

Taking it for granted that like most other entrepreneurs he'll eventually get itchy and feel compelled to turn new ideas into realities, Aaron remembers assuming as a young man "that when you reach some point in the future, what it is you're supposed to do will just magically appear to you. I'm afraid I still haven't reached that point."

"Some things are a bit more clear. I get more and more excited about caring for and raising my family, raising a Godly son, raising a legacy, and instilling values in him, and that gives me an awful lot of purpose and direction moving forward vocationally. I realize sometimes that requires day-by-day, week-by-week, or year-by-year decisions, and right now my focus is on building a family more than anything else."

A SUCCESSFUL LIFE *is one that makes you truly happy. Often in America the term "successful" means you need to have a high paying job, big house, and nice (expensive) cars. I believe that if people feel they and their families would be more satisfied with a more meaningful job that pays less—thereby making them more content with a smaller house and car (or perhaps no car at all)— they should not sacrifice the contentment and happiness that comes with it, simply for the views of outsiders. If you are happy in what you are contributing to the world, then the world is that much of a better place for it.*

7

In the Navy Now

SHANNON CAVIN

Born: March 19, 1978; Ocean Springs, Mississippi
Homeschooling: 1992–1996
Family: Parents—Donald and Joy (divorced); Siblings—Kyle (18), Courtney (15)
Most memorable wisdom about life or learning: If I ever said I couldn't do it, my mom always said I could.
Favorite study: Early years—space and astronauts; Middle years—same and ballet lessons; Teen years—space and astronauts, dancing, scuba diving
Current work: U.S. Navy airman apprentice at the Defense Language Institute (since 1999)

She has loved the water for as long as she can remember, so it's understandable that now that Shannon has moved from Snellville, Georgia, to Monterey, California, she finds it "gorgeous." Assigned by the U.S. Navy to study Korean at the armed forces Defense Language Institute there, Shannon is a young woman who has, for a long time, been determined to carve out her own life path. She once spent 2 years convincing her mother to homeschool before she was able to leave a small Catholic school she had attended through eighth grade and come home for schooling.

Finding a Homeschooling Fit

Shannon first heard about homeschooling from a classmate who had previously learned at home. "She constantly talked about how much she hated school," says Shannon, "but she was so smart! I wondered how she knew all this stuff because my picture of homeschooling was to play around all day. She told me what her family did, and I thought it sounded great because you don't have to worry about all the jokers in class."

Shannon's constant urgings toward homeschooling opened Joy's mind enough for her to become increasingly aggravated by complaints from the school about Shannon's younger brothers Kyle and Courtney. "Neither of them liked paying attention," Shannon says. "The school was saying they needed to do math in a certain way— their way. Mom didn't really see the point if they were coming to the right conclusion in their own way, which they were. After a while, it all just got to her." Shannon's seeds of homeschooling had sprouted. Kyle and Courtney came home, followed by Shannon just a few months later. Joy thought she should finish the eighth grade, as a "closure point," and Shannon did so.

Shannon wasn't experiencing any problems at school, but she *was* working hard at an activity she loved and began at the age of 2—

ballet. "Once you get to a certain level that's your life, that's what you do," she explains. "I was dancing 35 to 40 hours a week with the Gwinnett Ballet Theater. Then I had rehearsals during the Christmas season and in the spring. I was constantly tired from staying up until ungodly hours doing homework, but I was always working because Mom said I had to maintain A's and B's. Homeschooling helped because it cut out a lot of dead time and busywork in my day."

The busywork of school had always annoyed Shannon. "If the teachers didn't have time for the class or wanted to do something else, they'd throw a worksheet at us. It seemed so pointless and unconstructive," she says. "It got to the point that if we got a workbook at the beginning of the year that looked to me like busywork, I'd finish it right away so I wouldn't have to do each separate lesson every night. To me it was just stupid."

Joy initially enrolled Shannon in a Catholic correspondence school for which the young teen quickly developed a dislike. "It was almost like being in school with courses already laid out and you were supposed to conform."

Then one day Joy noticed Shannon crying as she studied. "I *have* to write this, Mom, but I don't believe it," Shannon told her. "I don't think it's right that the only way you can get an answer right is if you write something you don't believe. I can't do it anymore."

Joy promised that together they would figure out something else. As Joy continued researching other homeschooling programs, the Cavins briefly considered not using a program at all. When they discovered Clonlara School's "very loose program," however, they felt it might fill their needs. "Clonlara lets you design your own course," says Shannon, "then they give you suggestions so that you can pursue things you're really interested in."

> **"If the teachers didn't have time for the class or wanted to do something else, they'd throw a worksheet at us. It seemed so pointless."**

> **While Shannon notes she rarely got sick after she began learning at home, the health benefits were more noticeable with Courtney.**

Because Kyle and Courtney were younger, Joy spent more time directly involved with their studies. Shannon, now high-school age, took a more self-directed route. "I needed the most discipline to get through the math I hated so much, so I'd usually start with that for about an hour around 9 A.M.," she explains. "Then I'd study three or four other subjects for about an hour apiece. With a nice time off for lunch, I'd be finished by 1 or 2 P.M."

"Afternoons were mine," Shannon continues, "because I didn't have to worry about 'homework.' Sometimes I'd take a nap, or go outside and run around in the forest for a while. I loved it that I could decide what courses I'd take, and that Mom and I could compare opinions on how well *we* thought I was doing in my studies. I had control over how much I could learn. There may be people who try to do as little as possible while homeschooling, but why rob yourself when there's so much to learn and you can learn what you want? It's fun, it's exciting, and you can enjoy it so much."

Like many other homeschooled students, Shannon quickly realized another personal benefit. "In school I did have some good teachers I really liked, but there you have to go through subjects at the same speed as everyone else in the class. You might get one chapter quickly and the next might take you longer, but for someone else it may be the other way around. That results in many not understanding something as well as they might," Shannon says. "At home there's a tailoring of learning so you wind up with a better understanding of what you're studying."

Health is another area favorably affected by homeschooling. While Shannon notes she rarely got sick after she began learning at home, the health benefits were more noticeable with Courtney. He was repeatedly sick while attending school, once missing several weeks in the course of a single year. The number of times he got sick once he became a homeschooler drastically reduced.

The Clonlara School program requires 300 hours of volunteer time, which Shannon filled with free baby-sitting and visits to nursing homes. She fell in love with the children she baby-sat as the family grew from three to five children. She was deeply touched by the response from the senior citizens with whom she spent time performing light household duties or, more often, just talking and listening. "That they have somebody there to actually care about them means so much to them," she recalls, "it almost made me cry many times."

As a teenager, Shannon also sent monthly donations to the Christian Children's Fund, helping to provide a Mexican child with food and shelter. She earned the money working as a receptionist in a doctor's office. At first, she simply utilized the extra afternoon time available because of homeschooling for the job, but her employer soon asked her to come on full time. Then Shannon earned money most of the day and completed bookwork in the evenings.

It was hard for Shannon when, at age 16, she gave up the ballet she had loved and practiced for so many years, especially after spending that summer studying with the Boston Ballet. But she wanted to pursue other interests that ballet had pushed to the back burner and knew that she wouldn't have the time needed for ballet any longer. Shannon jumped into opportunities for camping and kayaking whenever possible. Joy, an assistant scuba diver instructor, helped an eager Shannon learn how to dive, giving mother and daughter a chance to enjoy diving trips together.

From Homeschooling to the Navy

Shannon briefly attended college in Florida, but family financial stresses brought attendance to a rapid and unwanted end. She decided to follow up on a prior interest in serving in the navy and see what they had to offer.

Even though she held a high school diploma from Clonlara School, at first Shannon's recruiter "didn't know what to do with me," she says. "He insisted they didn't let homeschoolers in, but offered to see what he could do." The recruiter took Shannon's SAT (Scholastic Assessment Test) scores and placed a few phone calls to superiors in Washington, D.C. He found out homeschoolers were still a rather new phenomenon but had, in small numbers, been admitted into all the armed services. Within a week, Shannon became the navy's latest among the few homeschooled recruits. She aspired to become an aircrew rescue swimmer, so she postponed enlistment for 9 months to train and get into shape, often with the help of the recruiter who himself was an avid jogger.

In March 1999, after taking the mandatory aptitude test, Shannon began a 6-year enlistment and the rigorous training toward attendance at aircrew rescue swimmer school. It was a long haul, but she made it to the night of "Battle Stations," the final event to pass before graduation.

All the trainees went to bed at 8:45 P.M. At 10:00 P.M., the yelling and screaming began. "From that point on you're timed and judged on your survival skills and teamwork in everything you do," Shannon explains. "We went through the whole series of events we'd trained for weeks: fire fighting, line handling, obstacle courses, rescue missions, life raft procedures, and more. In between events we'd run from one building to another in battle dress, often carrying a seabag that gets heavier with every step." Each time Shannon felt she couldn't go on, she remembered a phrase repeated often by her mom during their homeschooling time together: "Of course you can do it, Shannon. You can do anything you set your mind to."

She set her mind not to fail because that meant remaining in boot camp to train and test all over again. "You might say I'd already been trained to keep going and so I did," says Shannon. "The next morning I was exhausted, blisters covered my feet, and every muscle ached. I think that was when I first hurt my legs."

A visit to the infirmary put Shannon on crutches for 2 weeks. Her legs remained tender, but she ditched the crutches to begin aircrew school in Pensacola with the group. Within a week, though, her legs ached again. Then, during a routine beach run the following week, Shannon's legs hurt so much she fell behind everyone else. "I was disenrolled from aircrew school, much to my dismay," she says, "and began looking for another job that I would have as much interest in."

The study of foreign language filled the bill, and Shannon was off to California and the Defense Language Institute where she now studies Korean. "It wasn't my first language choice, but the study is good for me because it's quite difficult," she says. "I get bored when things come too easily."

One of Shannon's first duties at the institute was to take a test that analyzed her learning style so that she, like the others, could approach the challenge of mastering a foreign language within one year as efficiently as possible. The test revealed that she's an "analytical global learner." An analytical learner, she was told, looks at every little thing, and a global learner takes in the full perspective. Shannon easily explains away the apparent discrepancy in terms. "With homeschooling you look at things in the textbook, but you also look at them outside of the book, and through the eyes of a parent who loves you. You see things from all points of view. I try to be as open-minded as possible," she continues, "because that's the only way you can learn something accurately. Obviously my upbringing had a lot to do with it, but homeschooling helped."

> **Shannon credits homeschooling with the discipline she possesses to sit down and study—a lot—at night. "We learn 5 years of Korean in a year. You have to be disciplined."**

Next, Shannon was assigned to a group with similar learning styles, and study group experiences abound. "Our class is doing really well right now because we're all sticking together and helping each other out," she notes. She also credits homeschooling with the discipline she possesses to sit down and study—a lot—at night. "We learn 5 years of Korean in a year. You have to be disciplined." No one in the class has been given security clearance yet, and until then Shannon has no idea how she will be using her new skill.

Shannon is quick to note that right after she signed up, all the armed services further relaxed their policies regarding admission of homeschoolers. (It's amazing what a nationwide shortage of new recruits will do for the military attitude toward homeschoolers.) "I started a revolution," she says.

A Sign of the Times

Shannon's brother Kyle is currently in his first year of college, but younger Courtney still learns at home. Joy and her husband, Donald, divorced last year and today a custody battle rages. Shannon reveals an unfortunate scenario played out in far too many homeschooling homes.

Homeschooling has been legal in all U.S. states for years now, significantly reducing the amount of legal problems families used to experience. Notable remaining sources of trouble, though, are marital separations and divorces and their accompanying legal wrangling. "Dad never really said anything about homeschooling while he was living with us," explains Shannon. "I don't know if he's really not supportive of it, but now he's saying he doesn't believe in it. I don't understand that because both Kyle and I have done well in college. I think it's one of those bargaining things," she concludes.

Often homeschooling does become a convenient bargaining chip in arguments about support payments, custody, and parental responsibility. Many absent parents realize just how integral a part of family life homeschooling becomes to those most deeply involved in it and see it as the former spouse's very real Achilles' heel. The threat of a judge ordering children into the government school system strikes so much terror in the homeschooling parent's heart that this parent is sometimes forced to give up or trade other reasonable demands in order to continue homeschooling.

A sign of the times, perhaps, this problem prompted the publication of an article in the December 1996 *Florida Bar Journal,* entitled "Home Education and Shared Parental Responsibility." The article serves as a primer for lawyers defending homeschooling in court. In the article attorney Kevin P. Smith notes, "The issue of educating the parties' child at home by one of the parties may be a hotly contested issue and a more frequent one as the number of programs increases." Smith urges Florida's matrimonial attorneys to educate themselves in the state's homeschooling laws or regulations so they may "thereafter argue with knowledge the home education alternative before the court." With the incredible growth of homeschooling, it would be wise for attorneys in all states to do the same.

Bringing the problem back to a personal level, Shannon recognizes the negative effect on Courtney of the uncertainty of the future of his homeschooling, especially with both older siblings away from home. "He has a hard time with it," she says. "He tries very hard to keep peace by saying everything's okay."

> "I never thought of socialization as a problem. If I wanted to be with people I would go find people."

Now Shannon faces the prospect of what she will do with her own children regarding schooling. Among Joy's scuba diving students who came to her home in preparation for lessons or trips was Michael Jones, a young man with whom Shannon now discusses an upcoming marriage, children, and the future. Michael joined the navy shortly after Shannon, and he's training as a gunner's mate in Virginia Beach, Virginia.

In conversations about homeschooling, Michael has expressed concerns about social interaction, or his perception of a lack thereof. "I never thought of socialization as a problem. If I wanted to be with people I would go find people," says Shannon, noting that pursuing her interests kept her in touch with many people. "I was always so busy. I had a lot of friends in ballet who shared the same pressures and understood. After that there was scuba diving, and I still love being by myself. I love to read, *I love to read,* which is a solitary thing. I love going to a park and enjoying just being there. I love quiet, but I also like being with people so I'm not an isolated person." While Shannon doesn't agree with Michael's assessment, she understands his thinking as it mirrors that of still so many others.

> **"Parents are always the first teachers a child has. Why not continue that by teaching at home and continuing to strengthen that bond between you?"**

Whether or not their own children will be homeschooled "depends on where we are and what types of careers we both have," says Shannon. "Right now neither of us even knows if we'll re-enlist and that will have a lot to do with it."

Shannon is a young woman keeping her options open. It's 5 more years until her enlistment is up "so I figure I have plenty of time to make decisions between now and then," she comments. "I hope to be able to accomplish a lot of travel over the next several years. I'll have plenty of training from the navy and may choose something to do based on that. Then again, I may choose to try something else entirely. Mom always told me to go ahead and try anything I think I can do, because if you don't try then you'll never know. She also raised me with the courage to make my own decisions and hold strong to my beliefs."

Joy's inspiring influence in Shannon's life is apparent enough that folks tell them they're a lot alike, which they both deny adamantly. Yet Shannon remembers Joy's love of homeschooling. "She loved the fact that we were home, that she was the one instilling knowledge in us. She just loved everything about it. She had so much fun with it, and we were always hopping on trips to see strange things, whether in a museum or on a mountain."

Likely that attitude toward learning influences Shannon's final advice for parents today considering homeschooling: "If you feel that homeschooling is the best way to educate your child, do it!" She elaborates: "Parents are always the first teachers a child has. Why not continue that by teaching at home and continuing to strengthen that bond between you? A parent has wonderful insights and opinions that can't be learned from a textbook. A parent becomes a 24-hour teacher integrating schoolwork with real life. History can come to life with visits to sites or museums, and your backyard can become a biology classroom. The ideas are as endless as a child's imagination and, more often than not, the parents learn something new as well. To the surprise of all, you may find that school doesn't have to be boring. Learning can be greatly accelerated by interest and enthusiasm for what you are learning."

I DIDN'T REALLY *know what school was
about when I was young. I never looked at what
I was learning in school. I didn't know until my
junior year when I was away from school, came
back, and saw that, whoa, I should take the
classes I might enjoy.*

8

Olympic Dreams Come True

TODD LODWICK

Born: November 21, 1976; Steamboat Springs, Colorado
Homeschooling: 1993–1995
Parents: Parents—Dennis and Jeanne; Siblings—Chris (25), Eric (20), Scott (18)
Most memorable wisdom about life or learning: From Mom—Respect people, and if you start something, finish it; from Dad—Wisdom of the hands to be able to build and fix things yourself.
Favorite study: Early years—math; Middle years—math; Teen years—physiology and anatomy (as a senior)
Current Work: National Ski Team for Nordic Combined (since 1993)
(More biographical information available at www.usskiteam.com)

Todd is relaxing from a grinding schedule in his condominium in Steamboat Springs, Colorado. As we talk, he enjoys the energetic company of Telly, a 10-month-old yellow Labrador. Todd moved into the condo 6 months before, after living with the "awesome" Treadway family for 2 years. If Todd walks just 20 feet out his door, he can stand at the edge of a river, he says. If he walks 5 more feet, he can disappear into the woods.

Life with the Treadways, condo living, and a brief stint at homeschooling were necessities for Todd for the same reason—competitive skiing. For seven winters, he has been a member of the National Ski Team for Nordic Combined, which participated in Olympic competition in Lillehammer, Norway, and Nagano, Japan. Today he has his sights on Salt Lake City, Utah, 2002.

The Lodwick family is one of many who combine homeschooling and government school, depending on their children's needs. Todd's older brother, Chris, also learned at home when he, too, was on the National Ski Team.

As the four Lodwick boys grew up, the family lived just outside Steamboat Springs in a yellow house surrounded by hay fields and the homes of other families who wanted to combine the convenience of town with rural living. "I couldn't throw a rock to the neighbor's house," says Todd, "but I did hit it with a golf ball once."

Those who taste the homeschooling lifestyle tend to become eager lifelong learners, and that was the case with Todd. A few years ago, when Todd was 21, the family worked together to build another home. Far more isolated, it sits 22 miles away from town and is surrounded by national forest on three sides. Its distance from town and training facilities necessitated Todd's move into Steamboat Springs.

"Building the house with Dad was an apprenticeship," Todd explains. "We didn't use any contractors, and he was the job foreman, telling us what we needed and how we were going to do things. Everything I know about carpentry, plumbing, electricity, and fixing a sink I learned from him. He taught me, 'If you haven't looked at it twice you haven't done it right.' Everything from concrete to stud walls to dry wall to electric to plumbing to tiling—he knows everything." Todd adds, "It's a hell of a house." Sharing activities as a family is a hallmark of those who choose the homeschooling lifestyle. While the Lodwicks came to homeschooling late in their child's academic life, the joint activity began early. Skiing came into Todd's life when he was just 2 years old. Looking at an old photo of his family alpine skiing, he guesses that he was 4 or 5 years old in the picture. "Dad has my younger brother Eric on his shoulders in a backpack, and we're all snow plowing down a slope. That's just the way we were brought up—skiing as a family. We grew up on Dad's shoulders skiing. That has a lot to do with how I feel about my balance on snow, how I grew up on my dad's shoulders."

At the age of 5, Todd became a member of an active winter sports club in Steamboat Springs. Each winter, he and his brothers went to the club immediately after school. "That's just what we did," he says. "Our parents picked us up at 8 o'clock when everything was finished."

Todd recalls one of the club's Easter egg hunts, "when the snow was still white" and he saw the ski jumpers. On seeing them, he said, "That is what I want to do." He joined the Buddy Warner League, which combined practice in cross-country, alpine, free style, and jumping. "I fell in love with the jumping part," recalls Todd.

> **Sharing activities as a family is a hallmark of those who choose the homeschooling lifestyle.**

In the year he turned 15, Todd competed as a jumper at the national level in front of a hometown crowd. In 1992, a coach approached him and said, "Here, put on these cross-country skis and try Nordic Combined." Todd obliged him. He switched to competing in Nordic Combined, a combination of jumping and cross-country.

"I knew what cross-country skiing was, for sure, and I knew somewhat how to do it, but I had never competed in it," he says.

Todd grew into a healthy teenage athlete, perfectly happy with school, though he would have preferred to attend Lowell Whiteman, "a ski school high school. It was too expensive so I didn't go," he says. "They have a flexible high school program—you can complete it in 3, 4, or even 5 years. And they don't have any electives, just the basics. You don't have to take restaurant arts or painting or woodwork. If you're going to be a zoology major, woodwork probably isn't going to help you out."

Homeschooling as Freedom to Ski

This skier came only briefly to homeschooling for reasons more utilitarian than many people's. Todd wanted to graduate with the people he had grown up with in his class, but he couldn't maintain his ski practice and competition schedules and sit in school at the same time. He had to get some credits outside of the government system. It may be because the homeschooling decision was pragmatic instead of philosophical that Todd continues to put stock in government school's socialization approach. "Homeschooling took away from social life. It disappeared," says Todd. "It might be different with a person who's not an athlete. Then he would get to see friends after school. Still, who do you have lunch with? Who do you take a break with?"

Nevertheless, he adds, "Homeschooling did have a positive effect for me. Once I homeschooled, then went back to school, I found I wanted to study something I enjoyed." He expresses concern, though, for those who might turn to homeschooling, then come to believe, "Okay, now I'm home. I don't have to do anything." It's not a strange statement coming from a state legislator fighting to increase homeschooling regulation or crack down on "truants," but it sounds odd coming from these quarters. Since I don't usually get to ask those who put forth such a notion, I'm compelled to ask it of Todd: "Do you personally know any homeschoolers like that?"

"I've heard stories like that," he answers, "that it didn't work out."

As our conversation unfolds, Todd sheds more light on the role of skiing in his conclusions about socialization. "I didn't know what was going on at school; I lost touch with my friends. I ski all winter. When skiing was over, I re-enrolled even though I was homeschooling. I definitely had friends on the team, but I lost some friends I had in middle school who I never got back in touch with because of skiing." Ski training seems to have been at least as responsible, if not more so, than homeschooling for Todd's lagging social life at that time.

Skiing enters the conversation yet again when Todd shares why there was no such thing as a typical homeschooling day for him. "If we had training in the morning, I'd go train, come back, have lunch, hang out for a little bit, then go train again in the afternoon. Then that evening I'd get together with my tutor, Shane, when she was free."

> **"A lot of the things I did were on my own, and my tutor and I wanted it that way."**

"It wasn't a day-to-day scheduling thing," continues Todd. "I'd call her up and ask if she had some time. She'd say, 'Meet me at the bookstore at such-and-such a time and we'll work on it.' Sometimes we had lessons at my house. A lot of the things I did were on my own and she wanted it that way. I wanted it that way, too, until I got in trouble and I didn't know what I was doing or how to fix something. Then I'd give her a call and she'd come down to help."

Along with working with a tutor, Todd used Brigham Young University's home study program to cover the Colorado subject requirements he needed while absent from school. He wanted his high school's diploma, obtainable only if he took more than half the required courses, or credits, physically present at the school. An alternative, undesirable to Todd, was a diploma available from Brigham Young.

Todd met with Shane 3 or 4 times a week while he was in town. It sounds like a lot until he remarks that he was in town only about 2 weeks each December 15 to March 15. That Todd holds fond memories of working with Shane is apparent as he shares one of them.

"I had to do a 12-page paper on different aspects of skiing as my final project," Todd begins. "We sat down for 4 days. I was typing away, getting ideas, getting it done. We tried to print it out from the computer and—poof—it erased. Here it was 11 o'clock at night and we lost it. In shorthand we quickly jotted down all the things we could remember from the paper, all the things we'd talked about. We slept, then met the next morning at 8 o'clock at a gas station in town. We were there until 4 the next morning getting that paper done. I was leaving for a trip and it was due before I got back."

Ultimately Todd received nine credits for homeschooling in business English, developmental reading, and science. While his approach is at the low end of the spectrum of taking advantage of homeschooling's educational freedom relative to government schools, he still expresses an appreciation of being able to choose his own course of study at home. "Brigham Young provides a list of subject courses. I looked through it and said, 'This looks cool. I'll take this science.' I looked through English and picked the ones that looked cool. As long as it was credit in the right subject," says Todd, "the school didn't have any say."

Todd spent many of his school years having trouble reading. "I'd be reading a sentence and think, 'That didn't make sense.' Then I'd read it again and see I had changed the 'b' to a 'd,'" he explains. "I don't know how they'd define it. I couldn't read as fast as the person who sat next to me, but I never called it anything. I think it's a bad thing to name it, label it. 'Well, son, you have dyslexia. You can't read. You're going to be like this for a long time.' Isn't it better to give them a positive outlook on it?" he asks.

In Todd's case, a positive outlook worked. "It's better now because I've read so much," he says. "I have control over whether I want to read or don't want to read. I think it was just a mental thing in myself that I wanted it to get better."

Olympic Homeschooler

A combination of practice and a positive outlook produces athletes who excel. Todd shares that a person gets on a national ski team "if you're good enough. Nordic Combined isn't like basketball or hockey or football. There are ranks you have to go through to be invited on to the team. If you can Nordic Combine ski, you're invited to the national championships."

The U.S. Ski Team pays a national champion for his work. For Todd, that "barely enough to get by" check is subsidized by a U.S. Olympic Committee program for skiers, which compensates them an amount of money commensurate with skills.

To maintain top-notch skills requires rigorous training. Conventional workouts for Todd may include weight lifting, running, biking, roller skiing, and a bit of pliometrics (bounding exercise to strengthen legs). He participates in time trials four times each year and travels to ski camps at home and abroad, until the day, usually in early November, when it's cold enough for ski mountains to make snow. Then it's time for real jumps again.

Competitors are notified about a month before as to whether or not they will compete in the Olympic games. One month doesn't sound like enough notice to me, and I tell Todd this. "But if you've been

> To date, Todd has won three World Cup and seven U.S. titles. He clinched his first international prize at age 17.

doing the training," he says, "it's just another competition. I'll have 24 competitions this year. Now I'm trying to stick with the program that's been given to me—hours to run, hours to bike, when we need to ski, work on technique, and worry about the Olympics when they come."

> Having experienced even a small degree of freedom to choose *what* he wanted to learn, Todd makes the connection between the power of choice and happiness.

To date, Todd has won three World Cup and seven U.S. titles. He clinched his first international prize at age 17. "Todd's one of the jumpers everybody watches, even in training," says his coach Tom Steitz. Indeed he turned a lot of heads when his first jump at his first Olympics (Lillehammer, Norway, 1994) measured 92 meters. He wound up in thirteenth place here, and in twentieth place at Nagano, Japan, in 1998.

"Todd's getting more mature every year," his coach continues. "This is his seventh season, but it's not as if he's tired of looking at it. He still wants to be the top dog."

Todd's girlfriend of 6 years, Sunny Owens, is a fellow skier. The couple isn't engaged, "but maybe next year," he says. "You never know." While they haven't discussed homeschooling for the next generation of Lodwicks, Todd thinks ahead. "You never know what the world's doing these days. If homeschooling is the only way they could get a good education, if the school system where we live isn't good, if I don't trust the school system, if they were having a hard time at school, homeschooling would be something I'd consider. I have 100% faith in homeschooling, whoever does it."

For Todd, a successful life equates with happiness. "If you're happy and doing the things you want to do, if you enjoy the job you're in and you're making enough money so that your financial obligations aren't stressful, then live life, be happy."

What is homeschooling's role in Todd's life devoted to skiing? "Homeschooling gave me the opportunity to fulfill dreams I have. If it wasn't for homeschooling I wouldn't have had the opportunity to ski."

Having experienced even a small degree of freedom to choose *what* he wanted to learn, Todd makes the connection between the power of choice and happiness. "In this regard, homeschooling may be better: It taught me that you *can* choose whatever you want to do. If you're happy building wooden chairs, then that's what you should do.

"By participating in homeschooling, learning became more important. It got me wondering what I really want to do. I found some subjects I enjoyed. That's what I'm going to take to college. Now I know I can take classes that I want instead of just taking classes that I *have* to."

"I'm still not sure what I'm going to do after skiing," says the young man who has already been thinking about this eventuality for 4 years. "But I've been an avid outdoorsman ever since my grandfather gave me a .22 when I was 6 years old and taught me how to shoot it. I wanted to open a sporting goods store—fishing, hunting, backpacking—the things I grew up with. That's basically my heritage, my background."

In the meantime, the Olympian's training schedule continues. He's off to Japan, will visit Lake Placid, New York, for the Goodwill Games, then head back to Steamboat Springs for a 4-day break before flying off to Europe.

Todd is looking forward to the 2002 Olympics in Salt Lake City. As his mom always told him: If you start something, you'd better finish it. This Olympian plans to do just that.

WITH ALL MY *parents' mistakes, they always had the right intentions. They homeschooled for* us. *It was their personal problems that messed up things.*

9

Self-Educated by Default

Tracy Pizura

Born: December 4, 1962; Osaka, Japan

Homeschooling: 1970 to present

Family: Parents—Robert and Florence; Siblings—Charles (36), John Paul (31), Jade (30), Robert, Jr. (28); Husband—John; Daughter—Summer (4)

Favorite study: Early years—social studies and other cultures, reading; Middle years—science, Darwin's theory; Teen years—culinary arts

Current Work: Self-employed personal chef; Elegant Edibles Personal Chef Services (since 1996)

"I have a very unique story," Tracy begins from her Jacksonville, Florida, apartment as we settle in for our interview. As with others in this book, I'd called to talk about her homeschooling experience. I wasn't expecting a tale of apocalyptic visions, child abuse, and a family devastated by gambling. In spite of everything she experienced, Tracy gave me, as she has given herself, confirmation of the seed of self-motivation in homeschooling that has led so many to success. Tracy further provides a glimpse into how that seed also guides the human spirit to rise above adversity.

A Steep Downhill Descent

The young and growing Westin family lived in British Columbia, Canada, where Tracy spent first grade in parochial school. Father Robert worked as a stockbroker and traveled the world several times. He took the family with him on his trips—to India, Spain, Italy, the South Pacific, and more.

Tracy vividly remembers the night that changed her life. Robert sat her down in the living room to announce that the family was moving. "He had a vision that the world was going to end in 1984. The only way we were to be saved," she says, "was to follow his guidance. This was part of the reason he was going to homeschool us. The other reason—the good part—was the school system's focus on teaching to the lowest common denominator."

The Westins did move, arriving in the Bahamas with four young children in tow. "I think my father did something wrong and that's why we left," says Tracy. She hasn't spoken with her family for years so she may never know the truth. In a Bahamian school, she completed second grade before beginning her homeschooling journey.

In the meantime, Robert was making a living as an "apparent" entrepreneur. "He had mail-order clubs and different businesses. He'd promote businesses to other people, get money from them, the business would fail, and he'd have a new business." Not many knew that, at the same time, Robert was planning to gather seven groups of seven people to survive the apocalypse, and he was to be the leader.

Tracy remembers the impact of apocalyptic talk on her life all too well. "Try to imagine being an 8-year-old told the world will end in 1984, and you have to follow the path your parents have told you about or else the spaceship's going to come and you're not going to be picked up. Even at that age, part of me thought it was just gobbledygook," she says, "but when 1984 came around, I was living on the edge, wondering what if they're right? You cry, you deal with pain, you search within yourself, you ask other people for answers. You really don't know what reality is because you've had this information put into you. Look at David Koresh and instances like that. They all get an idea and manifest it into something negative."

> **She read aloud books such as Napoleon Hill's** *Success Through a Positive Mental Attitude,* **teaching her children about a positive mental attitude.**

With the best of intentions and trying to make the most of the circumstances, Florence began homeschooling by guiding her children through a lot of schoolbooks and providing lots of time and attention. She read aloud books such as Napoleon Hill's *Success Through a Positive Mental Attitude,* teaching those of her children who at the time were old enough to understand about a positive mental attitude. "It wasn't reading, writing, or arithmetic, and it wasn't part of a curriculum," says Tracy. "It was incorporated into everyday life and became a big part of my education. Mom was doing a lot of soul searching at the same time I was. Hers, though, was tempered by my father's control factor so she couldn't really grow to what she wanted to be through these books."

Soon there were five children, and Florence's good intentions began to deteriorate. "I think once she dealt with the fact that she was responsible for educating five kids and helping my father run his own business, all the while not having any support network because my father pulled her out of society even as he sheltered us because he was 'the king,' it overwhelmed my mother," Tracy says.

Eventually Florence simply bought books and the children would go through them on their own, at their own pace. "There were no limits," as Tracy sees it. "Homeschooling was a lot of books and pens and crafts and experiences provided, and it was up to each individual child to go as far as he or she could personally go."

Tracy chose to read, read, and read some more. "I believed early on the only way I was going to succeed in life was to just keep educating myself until I knew as much as possible. I told myself the answer was the more you know, the stronger you will be." Tracy needed all the strength she could muster as she endured the betrayal and pain of sexual and physical abuse, and watched physical abuse inflicted on her little brother, as well.

To Miami and Work

In 1972, the family moved to Miami, Florida, entering the country as illegal aliens. "My parents didn't know what they were doing with their lives and they couldn't support us, so we all went out and found jobs for some stable income to go on with our own lives," says Tracy. "My brothers and sisters started bringing home paychecks when they were 10 and 11 years old. It's hard to believe this could happen in the States, but there were people who took advantage of them."

"We lived in a hotel on Miami Beach," Tracy continues, "and back in the early eighties it was hopping. The European trade was coming over in droves so there was lots of work: restaurant work, laying out and picking up pads on pool decks, selling suntan lotion, all kinds of things. All the entrepreneurs on the beach were pretty much drunk by 2 or 3 o'clock in the afternoon, so they'd pay kids to finish their work for them. They were all opportunities for us." Tracy calls all her siblings hard workers and self-sufficient: "None of us have ever been on welfare."

As a young teenager living in Miami Beach, Tracy took note of frequent news reports about senior citizens living alone, surviving on Corn Flakes and often suffering malnutrition. The idea that they were left to fend for themselves and unable to prepare their own meals left Tracy wishing that there was someone to take care of them, someone to deliver meals to their homes. The reality of her own survival pushed the idea to a back burner.

Robert and Florence entertained often when the money was flowing, and Tracy frequently cooked for their guests. Comfortable and confident with food preparation, she turned to the restaurant right next door to her "home" in the hotel for her first job. Tracy became a waitress.

"By waitressing, I learned the workings of the restaurant business," she says. "I dissected it. Since I never had a formal education, I didn't look at being in a suit and tie as acceptable, and being in black-and-white-checked pants and a white T-shirt as not being successful. It wasn't long before I was back in the kitchen cooking Hollandaise sauce and knocking stuff out on the line because I knew how to do it. I saw the hands-on creativity of it all and I liked it." By this point, Tracy's parents were addicted to dog track gambling, "obsessed with the system they created to win at the track. It still goes on to this day."

> **Tracy took note of frequent news reports about senior citizens living alone, surviving on Corn Flakes and often suffering malnutrition.**

After a couple of years, Tracy's feelings about her work pursuits changed. "I got into the mind-set that I needed to have a briefcase and be in an office to be successful," she says. "I became a fully licensed insurance agent, worked in a pawnshop, then at a Gap clothing store. I looked into fashion design, marketing, and administration. I went to career counseling and took tests to help find out what fit me, all for personal growth so I could look at and draw from everything. I don't know if I would have done that if I had gone to school."

"When I worked in the pawnshop, I learned about the value of things and secondary value. When I couldn't learn any more and it wasn't exciting or fun, I moved on to retail. There I learned how to do paperwork, and how they marketed, things like how different colors make people buy. It was just like the way I had learned in homeschooling. There, I'd read a book and learn about something, then go to another book and learn more—that's how I went through life. I took a job to make money and support myself, but I looked at it as a life learning experience."

> "I took a job to make money and support myself, but I looked at it as a life learning experience."

"I couldn't see going to work at something I didn't like to do, every day for 30 years only to retire, doing the same thing every day and never growing as a person," Tracy continues. "To me that's a waste of life. I've been broke, I've been bankrupt, I've counted pennies to put food on the table. I've had diamond rings, brand new cars, and lived in beautiful homes through my life, too, and what it all boils down to is the growth—what you experience, what you learn. You have to get up every morning and grow or else you might as well be dead."

To anyone who cared to observe, it probably looked as if Tracy was floundering, void of direction or purpose in life. For this survivor, though, the direction and purpose always converged into a love of learning and a burning desire for that reason to get out of bed each morning. This path, as many homeschoolers have learned, isn't always straight *or* well worn. At age 28, it took her to Hallendale High where she took and aced a GED (high school equivalency) test.

It also led her to a couple of community colleges, changing majors with every step.

The path twisted through the kitchens of some of Miami's finest eateries, and to bartending work at a Miami hotel where the management appreciated her passion for "thematic" entertaining. There she created additional bar business by preparing food for the patrons for "events" like Monday Night Football. While she tended bar one night, the president of Johnson and Wales University came in for a drink, accompanied by a contingent that was opening the culinary university's new campus in southern Florida. A fellow employee mentioned Tracy's abilities, and the university folks encouraged her to check out their school.

"Faith is a beautiful thing," Tracy muses. "People are sometimes put in your path so if you want to grab opportunity it's there for you. I never thought about culinary school before, but I just knew I could do well in college. I thought, 'This is what you need to do.' I didn't know what I'd do with it after graduation, but I knew I wanted to grow and learn so I went for it."

The new campus had its first enrollee—a now 29-year-old Tracy. She found herself in on the ground floor of a culinary school's development. "I did volunteer work for them while I was there," she says. "It was a friendship thing and a terrific learning experience. I never felt like I was going to school, even when I was going to school! I was 'behind the scenes' involved."

Tracy financed it all herself and graduated with a 4.0 average in 1994. "I've got student loans deferred for the rest of my life," she jokes. "I got financed, I worked and supported myself, I bought a car, I just did it. I wanted to achieve it for myself. The degree is packed away in a box somewhere. I have a big trophy that says 'President's Award,' which is the highest award the school bestows. It's sitting on a shelf. It could be packed away; it wouldn't affect me. I had to do it for me, and to prove to the world I could."

Do What You Love

Now a culinary school graduate who knew what she loved to do, Tracy recalled her teen idea of creating meals for delivery to people's homes. "I just kept searching for the answers until I found other people who had designed a personal chef business in California and across the country," she says. "There was actually someone else doing something similar to my idea! I networked and networked. It's an Anthony Robbins idea—you put an idea out there and your thoughts become your reality." In 1996, Elegant Edibles Personal Chef Services was born, 3 years before *Entrepreneur Magazine* called personal chefs "the hottest business for 1999."

"I'm one of those fortunates," Tracy says. "Cooking is now my business, but it's also my love." She also works with the other loves of her life, husband John and young daughter Summer, who can be there because Mom works from home.

John was a fellow restaurant manager when the couple met shortly after Tracy's college graduation. "We talked about everything and realized we shared a lot of the same dreams and goals," remembers Tracy. "We went from working together, opening a restaurant together, and spending a lot of time together to having a family.

"John was very impressed with the idea when I first told him about homeschooling," Tracy continues. "He felt what he got out of schools left him handicapped in a lot of things and he wasn't successful. As a result, I left my previous career to stay home with Summer, and we've never put her in day care. Our family members don't understand why I don't just work so we can have two cars and a big fat bank account. They don't understand I only really have one chance to guide Summer, and whatever I do then is going to be what I leave behind. No matter what happened financially, no matter what happened in any other aspect of my life, my priority was our daughter and I believed everything else would fall into place, which it has. Homeschooling starts at birth and there's no beginning or end to it. John feels the same way, too."

Financial problems did hit the Pizuras in the form of personal bankruptcy. Today, John holds down two jobs in the restaurant industry, helps with jobs for Elegant Edibles, and serves as a trusted sounding board for Tracy. Their bankruptcy is 2 years old, and the couple can today be spotted sporting around in a "new" used Elegant Edibles van.

John's a partner in something else, too—homeschooling with Summer. "He sits with her and helps with her ABCs and those things. He has a different approach than I do," explains Tracy, "and I want her to learn from both of us. He teaches, corrects, and motivates very differently than I do. My mother was a perfectionist and very demanding, and I find I expect too much of Summer sometimes. I don't criticize a lot, but at times I have to remember to hold back on that. John's approach is more like a game. The instructions will say 'color this' and he'll tell her to put 'X's.' I'll say, 'It's got to be the way the instructions say.' I think she's going to get a very good balance. Homeschooling works best when it's a family affair. Part of the problem with my mother and father was the responsibility was placed only on my mother."

> **In 1996, Elegant Edibles Personal Chef Services was born, 3 years before *Entrepreneur Magazine* called personal chefs "the hottest business for 1999."**

Today, Tracy fills spare time with sewing, crocheting, visiting the library to satisfy her love of reading, and working in her herb garden, the bounty of which she uses in her business. Two of her brothers "haven't done much with their lives." Younger sister Jade works in day care and attends school in the hopes of opening her own day care center. Her brother John also graduated from college with a 4.0 GPA and works for Lucent Technologies. Tracy believes that given her family's circumstances, the children who enjoyed learning are successful today, and the ones who didn't, aren't. Bottom line, says Tracy, it all depended on individual self-motivation.

I personally can't imagine a gal like Tracy ever feeling comfortable sending her child to government school. "People want others to make their decisions for them because it takes the fear and responsibility out of it," she declares. "When you decide to homeschool, you take that fear and responsibility back on your shoulders."

"If I had to live my life over again," she muses, "with all the abuse and pain I've gone through, and all the happiness, too, I probably wouldn't change a thing because my experiences have brought me to the point I'm at today. If I went back and took out only the factor of homeschooling and I went to school instead, I would never have the insight and the wisdom I have today. I didn't follow a structured path and that was a positive thing for me. I would choose it again, even with all the negatives."

> "I found what I like to do, then found a way to make money by doing it. It was important for me to be happy first and the money would follow."

A successful life, according to Tracy, is one in which someone lives life the way she does. "I love to cook. I love people. I love making people happy and sharing what I can do with them," she says. "Their feedback fuels me, and I happen to make a good living at it, but I didn't go out to look to make a good living. I went out and found what I like to do, then found a way to make money by doing it. It was important for me to be happy first and the money would follow."

Tracy plans to keep growing personally and in her marriage. "I plan to guide my daughter and give her the resources so she can become the best person she can be. I hope to have the wisdom to see what *she* wants to do, not what I want her to do. I want to give her a great example."

Most homeschooling moms are full of advice on the topic. Since homeschooling bends to fit the personalities involved, each practitioner offers a unique perspective. I was eager to hear Tracy's. "If I could give advice to anybody thinking about homeschooling, I would tell them, #1, never get your children to approach learning as a task or something they would dread or not want to do," Tracy begins. "Incorporate learning as living. Once the children grasp that perception of learning they will never limit themselves. You always want to live, and to live is learning. #2, read. Teach your children how to read. Provide them with books. If I hadn't learned how to read, I would never be where I am today. Reading saved me, reading about other people who came from *terrible* childhoods that make mine seem like a walk in the park. Learning about these other people helped me better deal with what I've been through. Give your children the gift of a love of reading."

"I want to tell my story," says Tracy. "I don't want to go into graphic details about the negative. I want to tell my story in a positive light so it can help other people."

I think you just did, Tracy. Thank you.

I THINK I *always educated myself. Since I started working at the age of 8, I wasn't in school that much, so I realized that my life had to be my school, my whole life had to be my education.*

10

On Broadway

ELAN RIVERA

Born: June 11, 1981; New York City
Homeschooling: 1997–1999
Family: Parents—Victor and Taunya ("happily divorced")
Most memorable wisdom about life or learning: Try hard and you'll accomplish it.
Favorite study: Early years—singing Patti LaBelle and Michael Jackson music, puzzles, acting; Middle years—same; Teen years—world history; travel to Europe, Japan, South America, Central America
Current work: Touring worldwide with singing group DLG (Dark Latin Groove)

Think about life in New York City and it conjures up unlimited choices in lifestyle, friends, food, entertainment, and tourist attractions. For Taunya Rivera, it also meant choice in schools for her active, "overly talkative" little girl, Elan, from the time she was 2 years old. "I would change her school if it wasn't working for her," says Taunya, a former teacher turned social worker whose self-employment as a consultant has turned into full-time work as the coordinator of a social service agency's teen abuse department.

As an early childhood educator on New York's west side, it was easy for Taunya to take Elan to the preschool where she taught. Due to Elan's health problems and Taunya's desire to spend more time at home together, Taunya next created a toddler education program in her home, a source of income for her and of friends for Elan. When it came time to return to school again, a teacher living a couple of blocks away transported Elan to the east-side school Taunya had chosen. The logistics were challenging for a single mom, but it was important to her to find a school that would work *with* her, especially since Elan didn't mind correcting her teachers when she thought they were wrong.

"Sometimes she wouldn't know she was a child," says Taunya. "She'd speak to an adult as though she was an adult. No disrespect; it seems sometimes like you have these little people who have been here before, and sometimes I think she didn't realize that she was small. When I went to the school and they asked if I was Elan's mother, I would ask, 'Why?' Should I admit it—or what did she do now?"

The lure of show business grabbed Elan early. At 8 years old, she was singing, dancing, and acting. Busy with commercials, jingles, voice-overs, and off-Broadway work, she quickly grew accustomed to missing class time and making up work on her own. As she looks back, she realizes this served as good, early preparation for the homeschooling to come.

To help Elan make the most of her growing career and to allow time for the world travel that was often necessary, mother and daughter next chose La Guardia High School of Performing Arts, 3,000 students strong and the fifth school Elan would attend. As a freshman, Elan took and passed all of New York State's Regents exams in the subjects she studied. "I even went to summer school for math when I didn't have to," she adds.

Because failing just one Regents exam precludes obtaining a Regents diploma (a big deal nowhere except in New York), Elan was determined to take them all. "I tried so hard to take everything in my sophomore year. I wanted 3 years of Spanish, even though only 2 are required. I took German in case I didn't finish Spanish," she explains. "I took a lot of electives until I realized it was too much. I couldn't concentrate on one thing at a time, so I just stopped doing a couple of things and focused on what the state of New York wanted me to concentrate on."

On Broadway

The self-imposed, pressure-filled schedule continued until Elan landed a role in Paul Simon's Broadway production, *The Capeman*. A long-term, daily workshop precedes each production, so sophomore year grew even more grinding for this honor student. "I'd be in theory class for third period, then run next door to take the Spanish test I knew was scheduled," says Elan breathlessly. "At 11:50, I left history class to go downtown to *The Capeman* workshop. I got home about 7:30 at night, and I'd either do my homework then, or wake up at 5 A.M. to work on it, and go to school and do it all over again the next day. It was tiring sometimes, but the theater has everything I love—music, acting, dance. I knew I had to do this."

> **Elan attributes a lot of her stress over courses and grades to the idea of going to college.**

Elan attributes a lot of her stress over courses and grades to the idea of going to college or, more specifically, not knowing how colleges would eventually view her as an applicant. "They say they're going to consider a homeschooler, but are they really?" she asks. "Can you prove your point by saying, 'Well, the national spelling bee champion was a homeschooler!'"

When Elan's junior year started, work on *The Capeman* continued. "But I realized there were some people in that school that put my getting ready to work on Broadway in the same category as someone going to work at McDonald's," Elan explains. "I felt like I was doing something great for myself and my career and what I wanted in the future. Here I was in a performing school, and they just didn't dig it. Then I learned that the only people who were supporting me, my grade guide and theory teacher particularly, were leaving."

Timing is everything. One morning, Taunya turned on the morning news program *Good Day, New York* only to catch a short piece on homeschooling. She scrambled for a piece of paper to write down a phone number for more information. When she called, she learned about Michigan's Clonlara School, a time-honored homeschooling program that would provide curriculum, support, and yet another diploma for Elan. "This is it!" shouted Taunya when she learned Clonlara's roster included other students just like Elan whose schedules required the flexibility to take time off for travel and work.

It was time for Elan to come home, home to an educational approach that allowed the energetic teenager to continue her education *and* pursue her career dreams. "I had a lot of friends at school," says Elan, "and I had to leave them. I figured I'd make new friends in *The Capeman* and I'd keep my old ones. I knew that even though I was homeschooling, I was going to do well."

Homeschooling took on yet another of its many faces with Elan. "In the beginning—which was not like the end—I had tutors!" she exclaims. "Several of them taught multiple subjects, and they were a great thing for me, provided by On Location Education through *The Capeman* production company. This approach was almost like school, so it was a very easy transition. They gave report cards and assigned homework. I did academics in the morning and worked on *The Capeman* in the afternoon. The flow of it was easy and very scheduled."

Homeschooling Herself

Despite all the hard work, The Capeman didn't survive Broadway very long. "Once there are no more rehearsals," says Elan, "there go your tutors." She began to worry about the chemistry she wanted to learn, so "I decided to pay the tutor myself which was expensive—$50 an hour—but I think even that might be a deal," she adds.

Elan had previously worked so hard at her studies that now she only needed to study U.S. history and an English course to take the remaining Regents exams toward her Regents diploma. Without the tutors, "my regu-lar schedule disappeared," she says. "I started doing things differently every day practically. I'd study U.S. history for 4 hours one day and then not pick it up again for 2 weeks. I'd study something else for hours, or I'd study for 5 minutes, leave it alone, and come back to it. I had a lot of interruptions and days off for show business requirements, and I got distracted sometimes."

> "I'd study history for 4 hours one day and then not pick it up again for 2 weeks. I'd study something else for hours, or I'd study for 5 minutes, leave it alone, and come back to it."

With this schedule, Elan had difficulty gauging how much time she was actually spending on study. Clonlara had provided a grid sheet for tracking study hours, but Elan didn't like it, so she designed her own on her home computer, one she was more likely to complete. "I didn't realize how bad it would be not to be organized, but it's still not like going to high school!" she says.

Taunya remembers the homeschooling years as a period of reduced stress. "Getting your kid out to school is a pain in the ass!" she declares. "Elan is a fashion bug, and even if she had a uniform, she had to change it for herself. This means you don't go out the door just any kind of way. With homeschooling, she could study in her pajamas! She could get up any time she wanted, and she started her day reading in bed."

"I didn't have to make up any more stories for the school's sake just so she could pursue a valid outside interest. To Elan, everything is a learning experience, even an audition." Unfortunately, school personnel don't tend to see a connection between life and learning, even when dealing with young people like Elan who had never heard a good reason for why a school building was the only place she could read, write, or learn.

While Elan had already spent a lot of time learning at home with her mother before they donned the label "homeschoolers," she notes major differences between the school-centered and home-centered approaches to education. "A school day is about 6 hours," she explains. "The capacity of kids' learning ability is extremely high, but people don't realize it. The problem is, though, what kid wants to be in a school that long and learn even more than that? They have to have breaks. At home I don't have to get up and take 5 extra minutes to switch classes. I don't have to go through 'Everybody be quiet!' for 10 minutes. I can just go and sit and concentrate on the one thing I have to do. At home, if I need something a little special, Mom is there— one person across from you who is going to work on your special needs. You can finally just say, 'Look, I can't do this; can you help me?' That makes a big difference. If you can't concentrate at home, you can go to the library. That whole idea is still the idea of homeschooling."

Travel is a natural fit with homeschooling, too. "I had been to the Bahamas many, many times," says Taunya, "but never had gone to their museum that was one of the first auction houses for slaves. When we began homeschooling, I became much more aware of how there are educational places everywhere, and how you can take that in."

Many independent homeschoolers do volunteer work as a natural part of their learning experience. Mirroring this, Clonlara makes it a requirement, calling for a total of 300 volunteer hours over the course of 4 years. Elan chose to donate a majority of her hours to a New York City ashram with which she was previously associated. She began with housekeeping duties.

"My job was to take care of the library, which is equal to temple status in some cases, so everything had to be just so. From there I started getting further up in the housekeeping chain. It's a small ashram," Elan continues, "so they also use it for holiday celebrations. When it came to big holidays, there were always questions: Who's going to clean up; decorate; take care of flowers; give chocolates at the door to make visitors feel welcome? In thinking about these things, I went to the department heads and asked, 'Why don't the teens take care of this?' This was the beginning of the first teen program which I headed for a couple of months." At other times, Elan worked in the ashram's music department, sang for events, or worked with the younger children programs.

While working with Paul Simon and *The Capeman,* Elan participated in "Broadway Cares," an AIDS charity program. For about 10 minutes each evening after a performance, she ducked offstage after the first bow, changed into her street clothes, and held out a bucket for donations as theater goers departed. Just to round off the volunteer experience, Elan accepted opportunities to speak about show business at "moving up" and graduation ceremonies.

Elan completed the requirements to earn New York's Regents diploma, and is now finishing up Clonlara's paperwork requirements and exit exam, at which point she will receive yet another diploma.

Parent as Guide, not Teacher

Taunya feels her role as the parent in the homeschooling journey was a much smaller one than she had anticipated. It was much closer to a supporting role than a starring one. "In our case, Elan started with tutors on the set sometimes and a whole program laid out for her—what to study, where to study it," she explains. "The other thing is Elan is very good at talking people into things, like, 'Let me come and use your lab for chemistry. I can do it on my lunch break, and I'll sing at any of your functions.' She bartered. She would get free tutoring from teachers who had particular expertise and get into the labs. Even some tutors she had before, she'd just call them anytime."

Elan's learning team also included her mom, available whenever she was needed. Taunya discussed with her daughter how to go about assignments and occasionally offered comments on written papers. "I was more of a guide," notes Taunya. A Clonlara teacher was also always available to offer help via phone or e-mail.

> "Elan is very good at talking people into things, like, 'Let me come and use your lab for chemistry, and I'll sing at any of your functions.' She bartered."

The future likely holds college attendance somewhere in New York and a lot of other pursuits. "I'd like to be a lyricist. I'm going to learn how to sew better, and to draw my creations, too. I see a lack of fashion sense in the United States compared to other countries I've traveled to. The Japanese have great fashion sense. I want to see if I can bring it to America with my ideas. I'm planning to discover how to start new businesses that don't yet exist. I'd love to be an entrepreneur."

The future also holds a family, possibly with a current boyfriend who's also a best friend. "But we both know that I have to grow up some more," Elan explains. "I don't want to get married and have a child, even if I choose to adopt, and regret that for any reason."

On the subject of success, Elan has a lot to say. "My idea of success is not the 'I have this' materialistic idea; that's not what defines it for me. Success is when I look back on everything while in the present and have no regrets about what I've accomplished. Also going into my own mind and heart and knowing—not just saying, 'I think, I believe,' but *knowing*—I have worked for what I want as best I could. Success is also knowing you worked on your wealth inside and out, that you cleared your mind of the cobwebs."

When I asked Taunya how she first heard about homeschooling, she said that as a teacher she'd been aware of it from the beginning of its modern growth. Elan had started requesting homeschooling in first grade. The little girl who worked with computers and knew how to add and subtract before she went to preschool often tried to convince her mother that school attendance was wasting her time. Later, Taunya saw homeschooled children on the sets where Elan worked at the age of 9 or 10, but Taunya couldn't let go of the belief that a child needs school-style socialization. She moved Elan from one school to another in search of the socialization and academic challenges she felt Elan needed. It wasn't until she saw that the school schedule was seriously interfering with Elan's interests and talents and, as a mom, was convinced her daughter could handle schoolwork and a career simultaneously that she conceded homeschooling was a good alternative.

When asked if she has any advice for parents who may now be considering a homeschooling lifestyle for their families, here's what the mom of a child who had been asking to homeschool for a long time replied: "If your child really wants to be homeschooled, especially a child who has certain interests, you should definitely check it out. After we started, I thought, 'Man, why didn't we try this a long time ago?' I think it was my own fear of a big responsibility and a big risk."

Taunya recommends homeschooling to parents, noting that it is a path toward knowing what's *really* going on in a child's education through the one-on-one interaction it encourages. She cautions that for homeschooling to work best, parents shouldn't bring school home.

> "After we started homeschooling, I thought, 'Man, why didn't we try this a long time ago?' I think it was my own fear of a big responsibility and a big risk."

"Incorporate everything around your child into her learning," she says, "instead of just sitting there making book assignments that you review. Then learning becomes boring again."

Homeschooling has shown Taunya that schools need to change their ways if we are to stop making dropouts of those children who are either very bright and bored or who just don't learn in the one among many ways of teaching that schools use. She doesn't know how schools can accomplish these changes, but she does know that "kids *do* learn a lot on their own."

And what are Elan's parting thoughts as she continues in a life full of interesting pursuits yet to be explored? "Instead of wondering what I could take from being on the road or rehearsing and make it something good for class that my *teacher* would like, homeschooling changed my thinking to, 'What would help *me* become a better educated person?' Elan calls this a homeschooling-induced shift toward claiming her education as her own, the result of a realization that doesn't happen instantaneously, but instead unfolds over a period of time. She understands that there still will be occasions when it's necessary to please others. However, she says, "I have to impact my own life. I won't be living with teachers, but with myself for the rest of my life."

WHEN I WAS *10, I talked my parents into getting a small, unfinished dinghy. My dad said he'd get it for me if I'd fix it up. It was built, but it needed paint. I sanded the thing down and we painted it. We lived in Morro Bay at the time, so every day after school I'd take it out in the bay and go sailing. That was the catalyst that resparked my dad's vision to sail through the South Pacific.*

II

The Ocean Classroom

ROBIN LEE GRAHAM

Born: March 5, 1949; Santa Ana, California

Homeschooling: Off and on from age 13 to 16

Family: Parents—Lyle and Norma; Siblings—Michael (55); Wife—Patti; Children—Quimby (29), Benjamin (22)

Most memorable wisdom about life or learning: Discipline

Favorite study: Early years—drawing boats and planes; Middle years: sailing in Morro Bay every day after school; Teen years—pulling out of school and sailing

Current work: Self-employed building contractor (since 1978)

It's early in our conversation, but Robin Graham is already making distinctions between schooling and education. "From the school point of view, I'd be called a drop-out," he explains. "My parents pulled me out of school so I totally missed the eighth grade. I went back to school after that for one more year. I'm a pullout, there we go! As a result, I've never received a formal diploma from a school system. I don't even know if there was 'homeschooling' back then. There was correspondence schooling, but I don't think the term 'homeschooling' was even coined then."

Regardless of the name given to life without compulsory school attendance, an important lesson comes through clearly. "Education is really important, but also something you can do for yourself," Robin says. "You know, I probably have a form of dyslexia. I've got to be really careful about transposing figures, and I say things backwards a lot of times."

"The key to learning for yourself," he continues, "is knowing how to read. That's always been a weak area in my life, so it's not always been as easy as it could be. I'm a good reader now, but it's only been through years of working on it. Some people have a natural gift in reading, but we can all learn by practice. The more you do it the better you get."

Learning by Doing

Robin's dad, Lyle, who passed away 10 years ago, was a general building contractor for many years, so the family moved a lot. "He built a house about every 6 months, we'd move into it, and then he would sell it," explains Robin. "I think I went to about 16 different schools." Did this make it difficult to connect with the children at each school?

"No," he says. "Maybe if I was more social it would have bothered me more, but I wasn't so it didn't matter. Matter of fact," Robin adds, "I liked the changes, the new adventures, new places, new people, and new things to do."

Taking note of the problems Robin was having in school, Lyle chose for him instead an unconventional type of training. "Dad just yanked us out of school and that was it. He probably didn't say anything; he was too independent for that."

Thirteen-year-old Robin, along with the rest of the Graham family—Dad, mom Norma, and big brother Michael—packed and set sail through the South Pacific for 13 months, on the *Golden Hind* (a 36-foot Angleman), fulfilling a long-time dream for Lyle. At the age of 22, Lyle had readied a boat for a similar journey with his own brothers. The brothers' plans were cut short, though, by the advent of World War II when they all joined the services and Lyle became an army air corps pilot. By the end of their service, the brothers were all married, and they sold their partially completed boat.

> "Dad just yanked us out of school and that was it. He probably didn't say anything; he was too independent for that."

The family trip also helped Robin put academics in perspective. "That was our schooling for those years," he remembers, "eagerly receiving lessons from Dad in sailing and navigating. Consequently, I really believe strongly in education, but not formal education. Formal education is right for some people but not for all people."

"The funny thing," Robin adds, "is that when we got back from the South Pacific, Dad just enrolled me back into school where I would have been and didn't say anything. Nobody ever asked why I didn't go through missed grades. I just carried on where I left off."

Such adventures as a 2-year sail for an entire family need a fair amount of investment money. "Dad would jokingly say that he would retire now and work later. Basically that's what he did: retired, sold everything, packed the whole family up on a sailboat, and sailed through the South Pacific."

After the family trip, Robin returned to school, this time in Hawaii after he and his Dad sailed there from California. Robin remained in school for a long year, one that included running away from home with two friends. The trio planned to make it to the South Pacific, but were fortunate to land on Lanai Island after 3 days "in a 16-foot open lifeboat that wasn't seaworthy and nearly got us killed when we sailed right into a really strong gale." Robin chuckles. "It was kind of unrealistic."

It was realistic enough for Lyle to offer Robin an alternative to college. He'd loan Robin the money to purchase a boat and go sailing. "He thought there'd be a better future for me doing what I *wanted* to do. He could see maybe some future for me that way; he couldn't see any future for me otherwise," says Robin, now laughing.

And so began Robin's odyssey. "It was my idea to go sailing, and I think it was Dad's idea that I'd be the youngest one to sail around the world." And Robin just wanted to sail, so at age 15 he planned a follow-up to the family trip. "I was going with two other guys to be the youngest captain to sail a boat from California to Hawaii," says Robin. "I didn't mind using the youngest thing as a marketing tool so I'd be able to do what I wanted to do."

> **In what would have been his junior year in high school, Robin sailed off to become the youngest person to circle the globe—and to do it alone.**

A fiberglass boat company in Anaheim, California, originally said the young crew could make the trip in one of their boats, which needed to be delivered to Hawaii. The boys gathered enough sponsors for the trip, but the boat company kept pushing back the date that the boat would be ready. Some of the crew had school in the fall, and the winter seas grow too rough to sail from California to Hawaii. It seemed the boat company didn't want to risk the liability involved, but they didn't want anyone else to take liability or the potential glory either.

The boat deal fell through, but Lyle stepped in to help and flew to California to find a suitable boat. The moment in 1965 when Robin's school year was over, he joined Lyle for a month, and together they prepared the 24-foot sloop soon to become known worldwide as *Dove*. In what could have and would have been his junior year in high school, Robin sailed off to become the youngest person to circle the globe—and to do it alone.

Around the World

Newspaper accounts of Robin's adventures captured the imagination of *National Geographic* photographer Charles Allmon, a sailor himself who was always on the lookout for interesting stories for the magazine. Charles wrote to Lyle, and the contact resulted in three *National Geographic* articles about Robin.

The *National Geographic* waters grew rough, though, when during a stopover in Fiji, 18-year-old Robin met Patti, a dental assistant who planned to immigrate to Australia from the United States. Patti sailed or flew from port to port, awaiting Robin's arrival. When the couple met again in Australia, "We were at a point where we felt we wanted to commit our lives to each other." Robin took a break in his trip to live with Patti for a while.

"*National Geographic* came down because they felt this wouldn't look good in their magazine if people knew," he recalls. "They paid for Dad to go down to Australia and get rid of Patti. That put a wedge between Dad and me. A bitterness started developing. Patti and I wanted to get married when we got to South Africa, and at my age I needed parental permission to do so."

"Basically," says Robin, "I blackmailed them by telling them we'll tell everybody we're married and living together, so you can send your written permission or not." Robin and Patti were eventually married in South Africa after parental permission grudgingly arrived.

When the couple returned to California, Robin was barely out of his teens. "I had accomplished more than a lot of people throughout their lifetime of doing things. I got a full scholarship to Stanford University, I was awarded the Maverick of the Year sponsored by Ford Motor Company, which presented the winner with a Maverick car, and people wanted to put me on TV shows. By the accepted standard I had the world by the tail, but I wasn't happy." Indeed, Robin had returned to the States thinking that he and his father could let bygones be bygones. "That doesn't work in reality," he says, "unless you deal with those problems."

Robin was so unhappy that, one night after drinking too much, he contemplated suicide. He had a .32 pistol and was going to end it all. Fortunately, he didn't, and around that time his cousin began inviting Robin and Patti to his church. They took him up on one of his invitations and attended a church-sponsored seminar. "That was a real change in our lives. I needed to ask my Dad for forgiveness for being unappreciative, for being rebellious, for not being loyal." Robin followed through, and father and son were reconciled. "From that point on," he shares, "our relationship started developing, and before Dad died he was a real good grandfather."

The story of Robin's solo trip around the world still captures the imagination of every teenager who hears it, and is told within the pages of *Dove,* the most popular of the three books Robin wrote with Derek L. T. Gill about his voyage and life after the trip. *Dove* inspired a movie of the same name and is frequently found on school reading lists across the country, one of life's ironies when you consider Robin attributes the trip to dissatisfaction with his own school experience.

"My school experience was always very negative," Robin explains. "Either I was bored because things were too simple or I was way behind. Things just didn't click. What *did* click was when I went sailing with my parents in the South Pacific. I learned how to navigate and run a ship and sail, really very comfortably. So when I was 16 and left on my solo trip, I had more experience and knowledge than the average adult who goes cruising. A lot of people ask, 'Wasn't it a risk? Wasn't that scary?' For me to go out there was probably safer than hanging around and dragging the strip at home. But it was because I had an education in that area."

Robin never dreamed he'd be away for 5 years on his trip around the world. "I figured I'd just go through the South Pacific and go from there. Going around the world never really was my goal. It was just to go and see and travel and be out on my own. I did it for the adventure."

When finances grew tight, work-for-hire accompanied adventure. The article sales to *National Geographic* helped a lot. One time, Robin met Patti in the British Virgin Islands and they stayed for 6 months while he worked as a carpenter. The resort area, known then as "The Bitter End," boasts that some of Robin's handiwork remains there. Among his other jobs, he worked as a fitter's assistant at a power plant in Darwin, Australia, "erecting towers and things."

Apprentice to Life

Once home again, Robin took Stanford University up on its generous scholarship offer. It was there that he studied architectural engineering—for one semester. "I chose that course because I had a goal of building and I thought architecture would be an area that would be a good career. I left Stanford because I could see I was too impatient. They were telling me that after I got out of 5 years of school I'd spend 5 more years as an apprentice at an architectural firm—and that's where I'd *really* be

> I left Stanford because I could see I was too impatient.

learning the trade. I thought, 'That's a long time! Why not just skip Stanford and go directly to the architectural firm?'" In *Dove,* Robin tells more about his disillusionment with higher education.

One month later, in March 1971, Robin and Patti realized another goal. They moved to Montana where Robin worked in the woods as a sawyer (sawing wood in a lumber camp) after learning the trade in a college class sponsored by the industry. He found he was away from home far too often and too long, however, so in 1973, he switched to carpentry. He spent a year making furniture before he realized the area didn't supply a large enough market for his work.

Robin turned to building. "I didn't have any training in that field so I basically had to learn it on my own, and I did it with our log cabin, you know, cutting the trees, skidding them out of the woods, and peeling them. I didn't work for anybody else. I went to the library for trade periodicals. I got government pamphlets on how to build your own house. We got the very first issue of *Mother Earth News* when it came out. I talked to old-timers, and then I went back to the library again."

The 2,000-square-foot log home in which Robin and Patti still live today was the second of his early works, and the home in which the couple's children, Quimby (now 29) and Benjamin (22) grew up. "Our goal was to homeschool them," says Robin. Instead, Patti got involved in the start-up of a Christian school nearby, which Robin's cousin, who had a doctorate in literature, was creating. Quimby attended this school from kindergarten to eighth grade, then went to government junior high and high school.

> **Benjamin is a pretty social person, so we didn't think he'd ever go for the idea of homeschooling.**

Benjamin's educational experience was different. He went to the Christian school kindergarten, but then, like so many other Christian schools in the early- to mid-eighties, the school closed. Like many other families, the Grahams searched for alternatives. Their local school system was set up to allow parents to choose the school their children attended, so Robin and

Patti searched for like-minded teachers and chose various schools for Benjamin based on where they found them.

"By the time he finished ninth grade, we saw that even though Benjamin was a good kid, he was running around with kids who were also good kids but their value systems were different, and they would head him the wrong way," recalls Robin. "We took him to the same seminar on the coast we had attended years ago, and he made his own commitment to Christ at that time. Benjamin is a pretty social person, so we didn't think he'd ever go for the idea of homeschooling. But on our way home from that seminar, he said, 'You know, Mom, I'd sure like to homeschool.' He knew if he didn't break away from his friends there wouldn't be a change in his life."

So in tenth grade, Benjamin came home for learning. "Patti homeschooled him for about half a year. We went on a vacation and Quimby took over while we were gone. When we came back, she was doing such a good job of it she carried on for the rest of the year."

Since Robin is self-employed, and since he specializes in wood-working in the homes he builds, Benjamin had a state-of-the-art woodworking shop at his disposal. "One of Benjamin's projects in our absence was to make a big cabinet, a furniture piece. When we got back, he had this really nice iguana cage, a sort of antique piece with four raised panel doors below it in which to keep supplies."

Sounding the proud dad, Robin continues. "He had two big sliding glass doors where the iguana would stay. It had a little tray in there for the sand and a piece of branch for the iguana to stay on. It was kind of like an Ethan Allen piece, but a little more refined. When you build something like that, you're learning math, and so many as-pects of general education, and how to use your hands and pick out materials."

Robin is quick to point out that Benjamin never had the time necessary for such a project while attending school. "One of the things we saw when he was going to high school is that he would be at school all day, come home, and spend a lot of time in the evening doing homework, then go to school again. He'd have to spend so much time doing homework. During my boating days, I had met kids who used the Calvert correspondence course (prepackaged curriculum for grades K-8) who spent half a day doing lessons, were gone from school for a year, and came back ahead of their class. I knew there was so much wasted time and I hated seeing that. After that year of homeschooling, Benjamin worked full time for me doing carpentry work for 2 years. Then he went and got his GED."

It's been about 15 years since Robin has gone sailing. For about 7 years, the Graham family got into wind surfing instead. More recently, it's flying. Both Robin and Benjamin have earned their pilot's licenses, and Robin's future plans include flying for a missionary organization. Benjamin already participates in a 5-year program of missionary aviation, consisting of biblical training, obtaining an A&P license (airplane mechanic), and flight school, to obtain a bachelor of science degree in aviation.

In the past, the family has volunteered together on short-term missions to Israel, packing medical supplies for the Israeli Army, sleeping in the barracks, and eating in the mess hall with the soldiers. This was under the auspices of Volunteers for Israel (called SAREL in Israel). One of only a few Christian groups allowed to go in to help, they work to heal age-old wounds between the two religions by exemplifying the love of Christ. Robin and Patti may return to Israel again in the spring, unless they take the opportunity to visit on a sailboat with friends in Belize.

Currently, Patti and Robin facilitate an 18-week series of "practical, biblical" teachings designed to help parents instruct their children. And two big Graham family events loom on the horizon as we speak, both involving Quimby. After graduating as a registered nurse, she and her fiancé, a missionary surgeon in Niger, are getting married. She will move to Niger and practice in a hospital there.

Robin's solo trip around the world began more than 30 years ago before some of the others in this book were born. I wondered if in that time his own view of his accomplishment had changed.

"I don't know. The way I respond to people has really changed since having a Christian world view," he says. "When I got back, I was pretty fed up with people bugging me and people violating my privacy, but I see that was a totally self-centered point of view. We've met a lot of neat people who have been infatuated by the trip. Then there are people that I've admired. It's a common phenomenon: If somebody has done something you'd like to do, you want to hear more about it. We get correspondence from a lot of teachers who use the book in their classes. They'll often have students write to us."

I asked Robin if he has any advice for parents today regarding homeschooling, and he speaks passionately: "They need to take their children's education into their own hands, whether it's homeschooling, or finding a parochial school, or another school that will meet their children's needs. It's really the administration of the school. Not all public schools are bad, it just depends on the people in authority there. And not all parochial or Christian schools are good. You need to take your children's education seriously. Homeschooling's good, but it's not for everyone."

Homeschooling as both a child and as a parent has left Robin an advocate of apprenticeships.

Homeschooling as both a child and as a parent has left Robin an advocate of apprenticeships. "Ben was thinking about going into photography full time, so we found a local photographer making a living with photography," he explains. "And we arranged to have Ben go to the business and take lessons from him once a week. A lot of people who are good in their fields don't mind mentoring so the opportunities are available. In this way you're dealing with somebody who isn't doing it in theory; he's putting it into practice and making money doing it. These mentors have current contacts and current knowledge on how to market your skills. If you're going to be a doctor or some profession of that nature, you have to go through the run-of-the-mill educational process. But Colonel Sanders and Walt Disney did it on their own. Walt Disney went bankrupt I think seven times before he started Disneyland."

A business client arrived at Robin's home, and our conversation had to wind to a close. "Robin," I asked, "before you go, how do you define a successful life?"

"Success is having a right value system," he answers without hesitation, "having a family you love and who loves you—relationships. It doesn't have anything to do with monetary achievements because there are a lot of wealthy people out there who aren't successful."

HOMESCHOOLING MADE IT *possible for me to be different.*

12

Walking the Talk

AMBER LUVMOUR

Born: April 19, 1975; Carmel, California

Homeschooling: Birth to 1987

Family: Parents—Ba and Josette

Most memorable wisdom about life or learning: There are a lot of different learning styles, and public school doesn't address them well.

Favorite study: Early years—math (it meant fun things like baking, making patterns, measuring, and building); Middle years—horses, including riding one to school each day; Teen years—studying prejudice and inequality, pottery

Current Work: Program leader, EnCompass Authentic Education and Conscious Parenting (since 1989)

"When Amber was growing up we accepted a much, much lower standard of living, purposefully, because it was of higher value to us to be with her," explains Amber's mom, Josette, from the office of EnCompass, the Luvmour family's alternative educational business, in Nevada City, California. "The investment in a human being was greater to us than the need for a higher standard of living. Then, when she started going outside to school in the second half of her freshman year of high school, that's when we started picking up our worldly careers and increased our income."

Amber's life began far out in the Hawaiian countryside, over 2 miles out a long dirt road on the side of the Kilahuea volcano on the big island of Hawaii. There, she grew up without television or Barbie dolls. Josette and her husband, Ba, "were already alternative people in terms of relationship to social order." They were also both psychologists who knew what was going on in the government school system and didn't want any part of it for Amber. "It was important to us to allow her as much freedom in the development of who she wanted to be as possible," explains Josette, "and public schools do not allow that. They really do have an agenda on where and what they want a child to accomplish for proof of what they're doing."

At age 4, Amber dreamed of working and living with whales. Rather than attending school at kindergarten age, Amber loved playing in the forest with a friend who homeschooled with her. The pair climbed trees and created imaginary creatures. Josette remembers once driving them along a dirt road in the Hawaiian forest.

"Stop!" they hollered. "There's a ripe guava!"

"Where?" asked Josette who saw nothing.

About 5 yards into the forest, sure enough, there was one yellow guava on a tree among the many green ones. "That's the kind of vision they had," says Josette. "That, to me, was worth preserving."

While Amber has four older half-siblings with whom she maintains a relationship, she didn't grow up with them, so having a friend learn with her "was like having a sibling homeschooling with me," she says. "There were also times we had a teeny school of maybe five other homeschooled children who lived in Pahoa as we did."

Showing signs she wanted to learn to read at age 7, Amber's parents obliged her interest by exposing her to multiple methods of learning how. For years she learned math through cooking, building, sewing, and Cuisenaire rods (math manipulatives). "I'm the kind of learner who really has to get my hands involved, so it was much easier for me to learn that way," Amber says.

The Luvmour family left Hawaii for California when Amber was 9 years old. There "we began organizing the people in our community who had talents into what we called community-based education," Josette says. Unlike the method of homeschooling in which each family learns on its own, a group of homeschooling children "would go to different homes on different days and learn whatever that parent knew—herbology or sewing or glasswork."

> **For years she learned math through cooking, building, sewing, and Cuisenaire rods (math manipulatives).**

Amber enjoyed all of the activities associated with learning at home. "The only time I became unhappy was when I got older and wanted to be around people my own age. That was the whole reason I went to school—just because I wanted to be around kids my own age, and there weren't a lot of them homeschooling then."

Testing the Socialization Waters

Amber attended a small private school for the last half of seventh grade and the first half of eighth grade. She didn't climb aboard a bus to get there, though. She chose instead a half-hour ride on her horse who would stay in the school's barn with their horses during the day. "This was the time I studied horse anatomy, took care of my horse, took lessons, and taught lessons to younger children. I was never in big shows; instead I put on little shows for people I knew. My horse really liked to jump," Amber says, "so I would set up elaborate jumping courses and have my family and friends come and watch us."

In school, among her peers to socialize, "I got teased and put down," she says. "In my case, it was because I didn't have the right clothes, or I rode my horse to school, or I never went to school when I was younger. That whole part of school became unbearable for me."

Amber took it for a year and then returned home. "My parents didn't want me to go to public high school," she remembers, "but it was my choice and they understood they couldn't supply same-age peers for me. That's why we're building a school here at EnCompass—to create another option," she adds.

"Homeschooling is cool now. It's hip. It's in. Back then it was unheard of, considered weird or strange. I heard, 'Why don't you go to school? What's the matter with you, are you stupid?'"

Amber's words confirm the effect *on the children* created by hopefully well-intentioned, but ill-informed people commenting on an educational choice they don't understand.

"So actually that societal attitude had a strong bearing on your homeschooling because it caused you to pursue your education in a different way," I say, not realizing at first that I'm *telling* this to Amber instead of asking her another question. We're silent for a moment until she begins speaking again. She has more to say about the same-age socialization that was her quest in school attendance.

"Things didn't change much from middle school to high school," she states. "If I fit into any crowd, based on the clothing that I wore or my ideals, it would probably be the hippie crowd because I wore tie-dye and I liked John Lennon and the Beatles. But I went through my time in high school in every crowd. I was on the sports teams so I was a jock, but I was a preppy, too. By my junior year, it pretty much settled out that I was one of those people who was friends with everybody from all groups, but didn't really belong to any group myself." In retrospect, Amber feels this was a good thing for her, "and it felt good at the time, too. I was never caught in any of those social wars."

"Going to public school was a bit of a shock to her," says Josette who, as both a mother and a psychologist, observed Amber's transition. "Most kids in those public situations have been in school forever and they're totally bored with it. Amber went there excited and ready to take it on. She was met with a lot of established social cliques and rules and power lines." Dealing with the school's brand of academic work was easy compared to this challenge.

"We did a lot of counterbalance at home—processing, talking about what was going on, helping empower her to make the moves she felt she needed to make, or helping her discover what choices she might have in a given social situation," Josette explains. "At home we worked on the psychological-emotional level to help her integrate what she wanted to do. She didn't want us out there with her, but we gave her a lot of home support to balance what was happening out there."

> "By my junior year, I was one of those people who was friends with everybody from all groups, but didn't really belong to any group myself."

Josette believes that there was an additional reason that Amber wanted to attend government high school. "She set up her own personal challenge in her own mind, which was: 'Can I academically do what other kids do? Can I walk into that system and pull it off?' It was a family value that college would be worthwhile."

Amber stuck to that family value even though she was "pretty turned off" to high school by the middle of her junior year. "I strongly considered quitting and going back to homeschooling, but I really wanted to graduate and get a diploma from high school," she says. "I thought that would better my chances to go to college and that's what I wanted to do. Now I know that's not true, that I *didn't* need a diploma from high school, but back then that was the mind-set. I stuck it out in the only way I was able to—by spending as much time as I could in the pottery studios at school."

She found a strategy that ensured that time. The good grades Amber was accumulating in math class, combined with constant assurance to the teacher that she understood the lessons well, resulted in passes that let her head to pottery class to "catch up" on her work there. The tactic worked so well Amber expanded it to French class where her grades were less than stellar. Interestingly, it worked there, too. She'd complete assignments quickly for no other reason than to call them "done" and, voilà, she had permission to drop into pottery class to glaze, carve, design, or just talk with Mr. Rich[ardson], the art teacher. "It didn't really matter what I had to do; I just wanted to be there."

> "Now I know that's not true, that I *didn't* need a diploma from high school, but back then that was the mind-set."

Comparing homeschooling and government schooling learning approaches, Amber points generally to an at-home curriculum based on topics of personal interest, and specifically to a study of apartheid she completed as part of a greater study of prejudice and inequality while learning at home. "With Mom and Dad, I studied its history. In homeschooling, research papers *were* English class. In school, the approach was 'Now we're doing math. Now we're doing English. Now we're doing creative writing.' Separating all the subjects was a very different approach to learning from how we did it at home."

An Alternative Thinker Finds an Alternative College

With that high-school diploma for which she had tolerated so much finally in hand, Amber gleefully set off for Evergreen College, a Washington State liberal arts school named by *U.S. News & World Report* for 3 years running as the top public liberal arts college in the West.

"At Evergreen there are no departments, no prerequisites, and you don't major in anything." Amber explains. "You take a certain amount of science credits in order to graduate with a bachelor of science, but they can be in any sort of science. You might also get a bachelors of arts degree in the same way."

Even though Evergreen will allow picky students freedom to design and complete individual learning contracts with their teachers, Amber found plenty of existing classes she wanted to take. "As a freshman, I studied a lot of field biology and botany. For sophomore year, I focused on art and philosophy, then I took chemistry, calculus, and physics as a junior. I learned how to sail in the first quarter of that year, too, then spent the second quarter sailing from the bottom of the Puget Sound to the top of Vancouver Island, all the way through the inside passage." Amber chose observation and tracking of marine invertebrate life as her study during the trip.

It was as a senior the following year that Amber learned of an internship available with Cascadia Research, a nonprofit organization located in Olympia, Washington. She started at the bottom with menial chores but after almost a year, she was running her own research group. "I realized the dream I'd held on to since I was 4 years old," says Amber. "I was working with whales." They were gray whales off the Washington coast rather than Hawaii, but it was the dream fulfilled.

> Her internship was over, but Cascadia Research asked her to stay as a paid employee to conduct summer fieldwork. (Another homeschooler's volunteer work leads to a job!)

With all her credits completed, Amber graduated from Evergreen with a degree in marine biology. Her internship was over, but Cascadia Research asked her to stay as a paid employee to conduct summer fieldwork, taking identification photographs and writing up the research at the end. (Another homeschooler's volunteer work leads to a job!) "I worked for them for two more summers," she says, "until I decided I didn't want to pursue that field any longer. I had made my dream happen. I took a teaching job with a small homeschooling co-operative day school, instead."

After shelling out good money for a college education, many parents chew their nails when an adult child doesn't follow through with employment in the same field of study. Homeschooling parents tend to look at the situation from a different perspective.

"She hasn't chosen to pursue marine biology as a career, but to me it reflects a personal interest of hers taken to the *nth* degree. By pursuing that avenue she learned how to research anything she wants to know," says Josette. "The seeds of that started way back when she was allowed to just be herself without a lot of structure or demands to mold herself to something we needed her to be."

Adults like Amber and other grown homeschoolers in this book are precious resources. Many have tasted of the educational banquet available and can make comparisons that those of us who spent our compulsory school-age years in only one educational forum cannot. "I find the system is very limiting," says Amber, "and it doesn't allow one to grow and learn to her fullest potential. It funnels children into a certain way, and stifles them."

"Through homeschooling," she adds, "I learned you can do anything you set your mind to do. At home you can study whatever you want to. Good parents and homeschooling teachers fold all the different aspects of curriculum into what you're interested in learning so it's never boring, it's not horrible. There were some things that weren't necessarily interesting to me that I still had to do but, at home, learning wasn't something that was dragging, and it wasn't something forced on me, like learning how to do equations because you're going to need them in college. Dad said I had to learn how to type and I hated that, but he said it was a really important skill I had to learn, so I did."

Having imposed the same requirement on my own children, I brace myself and ask Amber if she is now glad she learned to type. She lets out a conciliatory, "Yeah," and adds, "By the time I got to college, I definitely used my typing skills a lot."

Different, but Interesting

Throughout her varied educational experiences, Amber worked with EnCompass, the family business, since its inception in 1989. "It was my family's lifestyle," she explains. "I wasn't told I had to be part of it; it was something I wanted to do."

Seven years ago a young man named Albee, the son of family friends, chose to work with EnCompass, too. The young people developed a friendship and took off on a trip around the world. While traveling through Southeast Asia, they decided to cut the trip short and return to dedicate their lives to the work of EnCompass. A wedding is in the works, and children are "definitely in the 5-years-or-sooner plan."

The "within 5 years" parents have discussed homeschooling for their children, and it's an open option right now. Amber says, "We'll have to explore more, but I would definitely say we'll be very careful. We both share the same sort of ideas about what we want for our children, the kind of environment we want them to be in and grow up in."

I asked many of the parents of the adults in this book if there was anything about homeschooling they didn't like. Many mentioned their homes now have a much more "lived-in" look about them, but Josette spoke of her fears about whether or not Amber would be able to measure up. "I wish there were people who had done it before me who could have helped me understand that fear was unnecessary," she says. "I lived with a gnawing 'Is she going to be okay? Is she really getting enough information? Is she really learning the right things? Is she going to be able to step back in if she wants to?' I don't know if this is a mother's fear, a neurotic's fear, or both, but there was an underlying fear about whether or not I was really doing the right thing. Now there's enough of us who have homeschooled for long enough that we can help alleviate these fears for new homeschoolers."

Josette was also concerned about Amber's small circle of friends. "If there was a falling out with one of them it impacted her strongly because she couldn't just turn away easily," Josette explains. "I think this happened because her circle was small."

Today Amber is a young woman who stepped out into the world on her own terms, experimented, traveled, and came home again to work she loves and believes in. Her self-confidence, born of success bolstered by strong family support, rings through her definition of a successful life.

"That's a big question," she begins. "A successful life is a life where you have people around you that love you and people that you can love. You have a feeling that you belong in what you're doing and where you are and who you are. You have the opportunity to grow and learn and teach what you know. You have the opportunity to be financially well enough off that you can support those things in your life that you think are worth supporting. You can make that money doing something you believe in doing, not just some 'job' that you have to do because you need the money. You have the opportunity to grow and learn spiritually as well as in other areas."

So what does a young woman about to get married, raise her own family, and continue the work her parents began, have to say to parents who today are sitting on the fence about a decision to homeschool? "I would have to know why they're sitting on the fence," Amber replies. "I would tell them to look at all of their choices and to really understand what their values are in raising their kids. You can't make somebody have the values of homeschooling. If what they want their children to do is be like everybody else, then maybe homeschooling is not the best thing for them. I would have them look closely at what it is they want for their children and try and pick the best place their children will get that."

"Don't be afraid of homeschooling because it's different or because you don't know about it," she continues. "Take the opportunity to really look at it and find out what it's all about and talk to other people. Homeschooling's not the answer to everything. Maybe it would be better for a child to go to a Waldorf or Montessori school or something else. I can't imagine it would be beneficial for them to go to public school, but for me in high school it was the only option I had to be with my friends. At EnCompass, I'm working on more opportunities for all of the kids. Come check us out. We're different, but we're interesting."

A LOT OF *parents don't realize how bad public school is, how rampant drugs, gangs, and violence are. I'm a police officer; I've been called in for bomb threats, fights, interracial fights. Drug dogs randomly sniff lockers and they've caught kids as young as third grade selling marijuana they got from their parents to other students. Too many parents have absolutely no idea.*

13

No Fear

KITTY GILMORE

Born: October 28, 1976; Phoenix, Arizona
Years Homeschooling: 1985–1992 ("graduated" at 15 years old)
Family: Parents—Tim and Sandy; Siblings—Carrie (20), Timothy (18), Nathan (16), Emily (12), Hannah (9), Alex (6); Husband—Maurice
Most memorable wisdom about life or learning: Dad taught me to take advantage of every opportunity to learn.
Favorite study: Early years—reading and history; Middle years—same; Teen years—same
Current Work: Arkansas State Police trooper (since 1998); U.S. Marshal (since 1999)

Second-grader Kitty's parents, Tim and Sandy, were as involved in their oldest child's school as any teacher or administrator could hope they would be. "We dressed up as Pilgrims. Tim's a good speaker and electrical engineer and gave classroom talks on the Space Shuttle guidance systems he works on," remembers Sandy. "We helped with the dinosaur murals. I sat in on classes and was the room mother who took in the cupcakes and punch and had parties with the kids. You name it, we were the parents who were there." Their involvement provided many opportunities to observe government school in action. These parents gave it a failing grade, and walked away toward educational uncertainty armed only with the conviction there had to be a better way to provide their child a good education.

Problems with Government School

The Malcolm home sat on the edge of an Arkansas town, rural enough to keep goats, chickens, and horses before a city eventually sprang up around it. The area's school was rife with discipline problems and, according to Kitty, some teachers who didn't have time to answer questions. She cites these as the reasons her parents took her out of school, but Sandy explains there were plenty of others.

Conversations with teachers revealed that the teachers felt they couldn't teach anymore because so many state-mandated enrichment programs gobbled up their time, and confirmed the Malcolms' belief that teachers spent too much time handling discipline problems. "Even that many years ago my husband and I were the only parents still married to each other, and the question the children asked me most was 'Where do you work?'" says Sandy. "And the chaos! Up for math group. Up for reading group. Up for music. Constantly moving from room to room, teacher to teacher—and in second and third grade. Kitty was nearing the end of third grade and her teacher wasn't teaching the math that we knew would be on the standardized test. We tutored her at home and it was taking all of our evening time to get her caught up. Tim and I looked at each other across the table one night and said, 'We could do this on our own in half the time and not use all our family time for extra school work.'"

Nearing her third-grade Christmas, Kitty returned home one day reporting that while the class made paper chains for the Christmas tree the teacher left the room. Two children started pulling the chains apart. Soon there was a scissors slashing "incident." When Sandy questioned the teacher about it, she was told, "I was out of the room. We had a room monitor watching four classrooms from the hallway. You know," she added, "when I leave my classroom I'm not responsible anymore."

This was the proverbial straw for the Malcolms, even though the principal agreed to put Kitty into a different classroom. Kitty finished out the third grade in the new class, and her last months in government school. After that, she came home, eventually followed by six younger siblings who "grew into homeschooling."

As fate would have it, Arkansas enacted a new law that made homeschooling legal. "Bill Clinton was our governor at that time," says Sandy. "We had a nice homeschool bill, but with political pressures Clinton enacted the stricter one that stayed with us for many years."

Free to Homeschool

Sandy had enjoyed 2 years of "preschool homeschooling" with Kitty's little sister, Carrie, who was learning how to read when her mom first heard about homeschooling from a pastor's wife. It looked like the perfect option for this family who knew private school tuition for seven children was far too expensive.

When Kitty came home (after third grade, mind you), she quickly realized her currently homeschooled little sister "was already two grades ahead of me in math," she says. "That was embarrassing. Dad had me go back to the basics since I was having trouble and I had to go through her schoolbooks until I finally caught up to where I was supposed to be."

She may have had trouble with math, but Kitty loved anything to do with history and literature's romantic period. "I read everything I wanted during homeschooling: *The Iliad, The Odyssey, Bulfinch's Mythology*; lots of mythology," Kitty says. "We'd go to the library and I'd get a grocery sack full of books. By the end of the week I'd go back for more."

Tim, with a family background of pastors and teachers, and known around the Malcolm household as "very organized," was in charge of creating the children's schedules each semester. "We started our day with chores then breakfast," Kitty explains. "Just like in a regular classroom we had an hour for different subjects. As my brothers and sisters grew, everyone did the same subject at the same time. Of course," she adds, "the older kids had more subjects. We had an hour or so lunch break, then got done about the same time as kids in school. After that I played," and Kitty relates with an embarrassed giggle, "and watched *Dukes of Hazzard.*"

> "I read everything I wanted during home-schooling: *The Iliad, The Odyssey, Bulfinch's Mythology*; lots of mythology."

As the oldest child in a full homeschooling house—one Sandy lovingly called their own "one-room schoolhouse"—Kitty often found herself in a teacher's role helping younger siblings learn. When brother Timothy experienced problems with math, Kitty played with flashcards with him, and helped him do drills on a chalkboard. "It took a long time but it definitely helped him," says Kitty. Her patience as a teacher paid off. While Sandy notes that Timothy probably would have been labeled learning disabled in a government school situation, today he's attending a technical college, pursuing a machine tool degree. "He made it," says Sandy. "I think it's stick-to-it-iveness."

Moving into her teen years, Kitty found herself drawn to collecting knowledge about law enforcement. "I clipped out articles from the paper," she says, "and read about profiling, just everything I could get my hands on." No one else in the home expressed interest in the topic, with the exception of baby brother Alex who currently wants to be "an army state police."

One day Sandy mentioned that the Conway Police Department was about to begin a police Explorer Scout cadet post. "I bugged and bugged her until she finally called to find out more about it," Kitty remembers. "I went to the first meeting and that was it—I was in. We had uniforms and they arranged for us to ride with police officers," she says. "I worked in every department so I could learn about everything. We could spend a week at the police academy every summer and experience the same courses they did. I got promoted through the ranks of the program. After 5 years, I was Captain."

As volunteers, the Cadets could choose their amount of participation. "In the summertime, I worked as much as 50 hours each week," Kitty remembers. "Every spare minute my parents would let me, I was down at the police department. I loved it."

Kitty laments that the post shut down shortly after she went into college. "I don't know why they don't do more of this," she says. "It gives a chance for hands-on experience, to try it out before you make it a career you might not like."

Not only did this go-getter use her time free of compulsory school attendance for volunteering in work she loved, she accomplished another goal she set for herself when she was just 12 years old. She completed high school at the age of 15, so she could move on to college. "Dad helped me study through the summers," Kitty says, "so I could just move through the normal courses at an advanced rate."

With her graduation mission accomplished, Kitty and her parents began looking into colleges. Information from the University of Central Arkansas (UCA) arrived, and tucked inside was a description of the Honors College, an elite college within UCA that provides a much smaller student/teacher ratio than normal. Kitty wanted to study in this environment.

> **She completed high school at the age of 15, so she could move on to college.**

Only one other homeschooler had previously attended Honors College and she hadn't done well. "The director was hesitant to take me because of this," says Kitty. In lieu of a state graduation diploma or a GED (high school equivalency), Kitty submitted scores of the standardized tests she'd taken throughout her years of homeschooling. She had also earned an ACT (American College Test) scholarship from Arkansas to cover her tuition. The Honors College director took a chance.

Kitty originally enrolled as a pre-law student, but changed to an English major, influenced by those who told her, "English is one of the few majors accepted just about anywhere because so many people today don't know how to write or communicate," she says. "I switched because I figured no matter what I did it would give me a good base." After 4 years, Kitty became the first homeschooler to graduate from Honors College, obtaining her bachelor's degree in English in 1997. Her sister has since followed in her footsteps.

While attending college, Kitty left her family home to experience the social interaction of dorm life. "I also wanted some space to do my own growing up and to be my own person without someone looking over my shoulder," she explains. After experiencing the dorm she was off to her own apartment. "Don't get me wrong," she quickly adds. "I love my parents very much and appreciate everything that they did for me during college. I've just always been independent and I was eager." In retrospect, she thinks this move put her in a "bad position."

The bad position was needing to work to cover her living expenses and help her parents pay all those college expenses beyond tuition. Kitty, however, had been a worker since the age of 15 when she self-studied cake decorating from books until she was satisfied she could apply for a job using her new skill.

Kitty decorated cakes and trained fellow employees for TCBY (The Country's Best Yogurt, a large chain of frozen-yogurt stores) for 3 years before working at a Kroger bakery part time. Much to Sandy's chagrin, one summer Kitty juggled one full-time and two part-time jobs, including working her way, as a 16-year-old, to Burger King manager within 2 months. The experience gave Kitty the opportunity to learn quickly how to work with employees older than her and who had been there longer than she had.

> **One summer Kitty juggled one full-time and two part-time jobs, including working her way, as a 16-year-old, to Burger King manager within 2 months.**

At 18, she moved on to full-time employment as a police dispatcher. "At first I was able to arrange my schedule so I went to classes in the morning and worked on weekends and afternoons," says Kitty. "In the last year and a half, though, I went to school during the day and studied while working the night shift. That about killed me."

Kitty graduated from Honors Colleges and leapt at a grant for a literary tour of England, Ireland, and Scotland. The trip provided credits toward a future master's degree. "It was the best experience of my life," Kitty says of the tour.

Homeschooled Trooper

With her family's encouragement, Kitty was one of 2,000 applicants seeking employment with the Arkansas

State Police in the fall of 1997. She was among the 50 applicants (which included only nine women applicants) chosen to report to a grinding 4 months of Troop School which began in Camden—"the armpit of the world," Kitty remembers—and concluded in Little Rock.

> **Was homeschooling an issue at troop school? "No," says Kitty. "Survival was."**

"I had some trouble in troop school," she says. "I love to run, but I'm not good. At school they set up running formation with the tallest in front and shortest in the rear. The front guys set the pace and I wasn't always able to stay with them. I did the best I could, but they'd get mad when they had to do push-ups because of me. A few men picked on me all the way through but I finally squared off with one of the biggest during the last week; he apologized and left me alone. I should have wised up and done it long before then, but I'm a non-confrontational person, if possible."

Was homeschooling an issue at troop school? "No," says Kitty. "Survival was." Thirty-eight of the original 50 applicants graduated. Of the nine women applicants, Kitty was among the five who survived.

From troop school Kitty settled into Faulkner County's Highway Patrol. Today she can be found in a take-home car (a state police vehicle issued for her exclusive use), "checking 10-8," meaning she's on duty the moment she gets into the car and sent wherever needed. "We do anything that comes up," Kitty explains. "We work a lot of accidents, look for suspects, and assist local agencies that may need help. We're actually on call when we're not in the car, too. For example," she continues, "my sergeant called Sunday around 1 P.M. I had to be in Little Rock at 2 P.M. for a manhunt. I was gone for 2 days working 12-hour shifts." (Yes, they got their man.)

Kitty feels she brings self-motivation acquired through home-schooling to her job. "Sometimes I won't see my boss for a week or two, so it's much like homeschooling, being diligent and doing a good job and working hard *even* when there's no one around," she says. "I see a lot of people willing to do as little as possible to get by. I'm not a go-getter all the time, but I don't believe in doing what I would call half-assed work."

Becoming a trooper is another goal fulfilled for a woman taught from a young age that any goal worth having is worth working for. While the job is something she always wanted to do, she's not sure this is *it*. "I have to have a goal I'm moving toward, something to keep my interest piqued," Kitty says, which is one reason she recently took part-time work with the U.S. Marshals. She's kicking around the idea of pursuing this full-time, but the marshals won't test applicants again until 2003. If she takes and passes the test it will require 4 months of school in Virginia and take her away from new husband, Maurice.

Maurice works as an investigator for the state tobacco control board. He thought Kitty's homeschooling was "neat," and it quickly took a backseat to the fact that she was a police officer. "He was the first guy that was okay with me being a trooper," she says. "Most guys got really intimidated by it."

> "I'd be hesitant to put children in public school now, not only because of the violence, but I feel it's such a zoo."

When the couple has children (almost a certainty), Kitty would like to homeschool them, even though she admits she doesn't know how that's going to work with their careers. She adds, "I'd be hesitant to put children in public school now, not only because of the violence, but I feel it's such a zoo. They give children so much busywork it kills their desire to learn. You see children get out of school now and they have no brightness in their eyes; that flame has been extinguished. Safety is a big concern; public schools have no control over what's happening."

Kitty plans to apply to the University of Little Rock to continue earning the master's degree on which she has a head start. She's checking into an advanced business program that will allow her to finish in a year and a half.

For all her accomplishments—and a schedule that would make most folks' head spin—Kitty holds a pretty simple definition of a successful life. "There's a lot of joy in having a family and being with someone you love. A lot of happiness stems from having a close-knit family."

"I had a lot more time to watch my parents' example because of homeschooling," Kitty continues. "Most modern kids get to see their parents maybe 3 hours of the day—maybe. I feel like my relationship with my parents is a lot closer because of the time spent together. It's gotten so much deeper as I've gotten older."

"I want enough money to be comfortable, but how much I don't care. The most important thing," she concludes, "is my family, being with my new husband, and whatever children we may have."

When Sandy began homeschooling Kitty, the family was aware of seven other homeschooling children in their county. Thanks to the hard work of homeschooling pioneers like the Malcolms, who still create the newsletter for their support group, activities and social opportunities abound for the 350 children of current members. Kitty sounds both amazed and just a little bit jealous of all the opportunities available to her still-homeschooling siblings, noting she sometimes felt isolated until she could participate in the organized activities available to older children.

Still, Kitty would homeschool again "in a heartbeat. Fears about homeschoolers in college are hogwash," she states with conviction. "We're not just interested in getting a grade. I was truly interested in learning and that sets you apart from others who are just trying to get by."

That interest in learning often affects the homeschooling parents, too. Even though Sandy is still teaching her youngest how to read, she's looking toward the future. "By homeschooling my children, I've gotten the education I missed in public school," she says. "I'm encouraged to go back to college, too."

SO MANY PEOPLE *have said to me, "But homeschooling is such a great responsibility." I say back to them, "But you have the exact same responsibility; you're just not taking it."*

I4

Homeschooling: The Next Generation

BECKY AMOS

Born: September 26, 1958; Akron, Ohio
Homeschooling: 1970–1976
Family: Parents—Lawrence and Joan; Siblings—Douglas (deceased), Nathan (39), Sarah (36), Benjamin (26); Husband—Larry; Children—Ashley (9), Douglas (8), Alyssa (6)
Most memorable wisdom about life or learning: Learning never ends.
Favorite study: Early years—science; Middle years—biking in Europe and collecting costumes from foreign countries; Teen years—cross-country racing, ski racing
Current work: Freelance writing (since 1995)

Larry and Joan Bangs' children attended government school in Vermont's quaint town of Bennington, just as all their neighbors and friends did. On one beautiful May afternoon their oldest child, Douglas, returned home from school with the schedule it had laid out for his entry into seventh grade the following September.

"The schedule said he'd be studying Vermont history—for the fifth time in 7 years," recalls dad Larry, a Bennington high school teacher who was working on a Ph.D. in astrophysics. "When I called the school and asked about it, they said a new superintendent had changed the schedule around. I told them I want him to know there's something beyond the Hudson River."

This wasn't the end of Larry's frustration. "At the same time Becky came home from school and we invited her to go bicycling with us. She had to call a couple of friends first. That was it. I said, 'If Becky has to have a committee meeting to make up her mind, and Douglas is locked in the study of Vermont history, we're going to do something different.'"

The Bangs family packed up and left the state's southwest corner for an area known as Vermont's Northeast Kingdom. Here they settled into a previously purchased 200-year-old farmhouse on 500 acres and self-sufficiency became the family priority. They chopped their own wood, grew vegetables, raised their own meat, and, without ever having heard the term "homeschooling," chose to teach their own, too.

Income was scarce. Larry tried to continue work on his astrophysics thesis, but it came down to a decision as to whose education was more important—his own or the children's. Larry and Joan chose the children's education. They were concerned about their kids' ability "to get back into the mainstream" if they ever wanted to return to school or go to college, so they spoke with Dr. Russell, Vermont's assistant education commissioner at the time.

Dr. Russell had been a teacher in a 1-room schoolhouse in the town the Bangs now called home and, for lack of an established policy, it was up to her to decide exactly what relationship the Bangs, as home educators, would have with the state. According to Larry and Joan, Dr. Russell told them that she knew almost anything they would do would be more than the children would get from the local school. A review committee was formed which, says Larry, "checked to see if we had adequate lighting and that the toilet flushed. I guess somebody looked at the curriculum we provided, but that seemed to be the least of their concerns."

Becky came home to learn at what would have been her sixth-grade year. She remembers, "We were all excited about moving to the farm and raising animals, and having our parents teach us. All of our friends told us we were crazy, including my parents' friends, and we sort of ignored them. I didn't question where I was; I was happy in school and at home. It's only in retrospect that I realize what I gained was significantly greater after I left public school."

From Farmhouse to Academy

The family rose early enough to get morning chores done before entering the farmhouse's classroom by 8:30 A.M. Caring for the 15 beef cows and 50 sheep was considered a part of life, not part of a curriculum. "We were expected to change out of our chore clothes first," says Becky. "We did science, math, and those types of subjects in the morning, then more of the history and English subjects in the afternoon. We were apt to sit around and take part in reading a Shakespeare play. Local artists came in and worked with us. We studied impressionist painters, then took a picture and painted it in five different styles. If there was maple sugaring to do," Becky explains, "we read Shakespeare around the arch [a section of the evaporator] as it boiled away."

The children could also step out their back door to cross-country ski on their own trails they set with snowshoes. The activity gave Becky and her siblings the endurance to become competitive skiers on the cross-country team of the school the family eventually started. "I also ran and cut, baled, and put hay in the barn for winter," says Becky, "and we were out in very pure air up there, so I think we were about as healthy as you could get."

Another local family originally from Norway began homeschooling and the two families exchanged educational services as their children learned together. This continued for 2 years until the Bangs took their second 3-month-long bicycle trip to Europe, accompanied by 16 additional children from all over the country. One of the bicyclists, Kerry Irons, was disillusioned with school and wanted more. Her parents asked the Bangs to work with her.

> "I was happy in school and happy at home. It's only in retrospect that I realize what I gained was significantly greater after I left public school."

"In order to help them, we had two options," explains Larry. "We could either become a reporting school or a fully accredited certified school. We chose the latter, in part because the Northeast Kingdom has had a voucher system in place for 150 years. It's worked beautifully, and they hate to have you know it," he confides.

"You see," Larry continues, "we don't have a high school in our town, so students go to any other school they want, and they receive money to do so. In order for us to get some tuition money, and so that the girl could get academic credit and graduate with her class, which was important to her, we had to become a certified school."

The family quickly fulfilled the requirements which boiled down to establishing a board of trustees, showing financial viability so they didn't close down in the middle of a school year, and passing a health and safety inspection.

Northwood Academy began in 1971. In order to avoid confusion with Northwood Academy in Lake Placid, New York, which carried a reputation as a boarding school for problematic city children, the school's name was eventually changed to Wildridge Academy.

Study at Wildridge was based on a curriculum that began with prehistory, "and in about 6 years came up to the present time in chronological order," says Joan. While there were as many as 20 international students in grades K-12 studying college preparatory courses at any given time, students were simply identified as being either in the "lower grades" or the "upper grades." There were goals to work toward instead of letter grades, and a pass or fail system worked beautifully.

Turning one's home into a fully accredited academy has repercussions. "Our children had to share their parents, their home, and everything else," Joan explains. "That wasn't impossible, but it was difficult at times. We boarded some students for a few years, but stopped when we saw it was taking a lot from our own children."

Annual family bicycle trips to Europe continued, and together the family explored England, Scotland, Ireland, France, Belgium, and more. Upon finishing high school at 17, Becky returned to Europe alone. She participated in cross-country skiing races in Norway, then worked her way down to the Riviera where she continued studying the French language.

Larry prepared the path to higher education for his students, including his children, by visiting different colleges and explaining his methods and transcripts. Becky was admitted to Massachusetts' all-female Smith College on the strength of her essay and interviews. "All of Wildridge Academy's students could go into wherever they applied, and carry on extensive conversations with the interviewers in a large number of fields," says Joan, adding that colleges were impressed by this.

Life After Homeschooling

"When I went to college, I think I struggled more socially than most people do," Becky says. "However, from my perspective now I don't think it was a bad thing, and I wouldn't trade that socialization for the homeschooling. I don't think it's a trade-off at all. I never did fit in, but I grew to the point that I didn't care. The whole social thing was so shallow at college; so much party drinking, and everyone did what they thought they should do to impress their friends. So many of them spoke derogatorily of their parents, too, and I didn't feel that way at all." She transferred to Williams College to receive her degree, spurred on by the attitude her parents had always shared: You can attain anything you want if you're willing to work hard enough to get it.

> **"The whole social thing was so shallow at college; so much party drinking, and everyone did what they thought they should do to impress their friends."**

"My parents demonstrated this by inviting people to our little school, like former Vermont Governor George Aiken, Captain Irving Johnson (renowned English sailor and author), Olympic athletes, and two Nobel Laureates, among others," Becky remembers. "Most people would not have considered it likely that these people of note would come to Newark, Vermont, to address so small an audience, but my parents asked anyway and they came. These people also repeatedly told us to follow our dreams."

The result is "a confidence instilled in me by my parents that I would not have had if I had remained in a public school setting," says Becky. "I was a naturally shy person. That shyness was exacerbated by the homeschooling, I believe. I had difficulty feeling comfortable with my peers, and in retrospect if there were anything about homeschooling I didn't like it would be the feeling of loneliness I had. However," she adds, "homeschooling gave me a confidence in myself that allowed me to feel comfortable with adults in any walk of life. With a variety of experiences the shyness with my age group also disappeared. I think it's important to go through a period of loneliness because so many of us never learn to live with ourselves. For me it took that struggle with loneliness to be who I am today. I think that so often we run from that. Maybe that's what more of us need."

After college graduation, Becky eventually returned to Bennington where she started a career as a *Bennington Banner* newspaper reporter. One of the people who read her by-line was another Larry, a younger one who had lived next door to the Bangs family before they moved to the Northeast Kingdom 18 years prior. Larry was visiting home for Christmas from work in Chicago and gave Becky a call. "Sixteen days later we were engaged," giggles Becky, "and we were married in 6 months."

Larry Amos, a Bennington high school valedictorian and Yale graduate, is owner and president of Monument Industries, a company that manufactures plastic bags. Today he's proud dad to Ashley, Douglas, and Alyssa.

As happens in so many families who eventually wind up homeschooling, the Amos children tried a couple of schools. Ashley began in a private kindergarten associated with Bennington College. The next year the program was full, so Ashley—along with Douglas—went to government school. Larry wouldn't hear of homeschooling and the family lived in town and not on a farm, so Becky didn't think she would ever homeschool her children.

Carrying on the Tradition

Rather quickly, however, Becky began to see that other things accompanied academics in her children's government school. "At every turn they tried to sneak in drug and alcohol education, and I was opposed to that. I felt I didn't have control over my children's education in any way, shape, or form."

Ashley came home from first grade in November with her twelfth sheet on matching upper-and lower-case letters, and she's known them since she was 3 years old. No matter what I did, how much time I spent in the classroom, how much I talked to the teacher, I couldn't change anything."

"Then Douglas came home from half-day kindergarten one day and said, 'Mommy, I was in time-out three times today.' I turned to Larry and said, 'That's it. Legally he doesn't have to be in school until he is 7 years old so he is staying home with me until then. We will do what we can as far as learning is concerned, and then you can judge if he's doing more here than at school.'"

Decision time came at the end of that year as the family sat down at the dinner table one night and asked all three children where they wanted to learn the following year. All three answered, "At home!" including 4-year-old Alyssa. Larry agreed. About halfway through the second year of homeschooling, Larry asked Becky if she could homeschool Douglas through college.

"Obviously he's now 100 percent behind me, as are my parents and in-laws, which is just a wonderful situation," says Becky. "I feel like I have control of their education back, and I don't have to worry about what they're getting when my back is turned."

> "At every turn they tried to sneak in drug and alcohol education, and I was opposed to that. I felt I didn't have control over my children's education in any way, shape, or form."

As Becky looks back at homeschooling as a child, she feels her family is closer as a result. "Even if my parents may have gone gray a bit early," she jokes, "I think it had a very positive effect on them." Today she stands in their places, the parent creating a learning environment at home, one of a steadily growing number of second generation homeschooling families. The experience is having an effect on her life, too.

"When we took our children out of school and brought them home my stress level dropped dramatically," Becky shares. "When I dropped them off at school I felt like I was putting them in jail. Although they didn't feel that way, I felt they were wasting their time, and that they were being indoctrinated with information I didn't want them to have because they are still so young. They weren't equipped to handle the information on drugs and alcohol. The school made it an issue when it shouldn't have been, and I didn't trust what was being taught to them."

"Then there's all the things that *weren't* being taught to them that should have been," adds Becky. "I knew Douglas was being labeled a 'bad boy' from the beginning of school, and that would only get worse, but I knew he was acting out because he was bored. My stress level was sky high because I was feeling so helpless. The only way I could help them was to take them out of that situation. My mother-in-law keeps asking where I would rate my children in comparison to children at school, and I tell her it doesn't matter. I raise them; what matters is that they're doing everything they're capable of doing."

"I truly believe that the rewards are now twofold for my parents. Not only did they watch their own children succeed, through school and then into life, but they're watching me make the choice to teach my children at home, making their success doubly sweet."

Indeed, life lessons learned as a child on the farm permeate Becky's adult life today. "It's nice that we don't have financial worries," she confesses, "but our challenge now is to give our children the same sense of urgency and having to participate, being a part of things, and working for what we have. At the same time, we have to keep it from becoming an artificial thing. I don't measure success by things, because things are so easily taken away. Success is what you have in your mind and in your soul, those things that can't be taken away, those things that can't be measured by what your job is or any of those artificial things."

> "I truly believe that the rewards are now twofold for my parents."

"We read about the Wright brothers, and I was so impressed that their father made them first of all figure out a way to earn the money to buy the parts to do their experiments. I would like to be able to say we do that for our children. I don't, I'm a little bit easy on them in that, but that's what we're working towards. I want them to feel that sense that if they want it really badly, they have to be innovative and creative. They don't just run to the store and buy it with money that Mom handed them."

By being willing to speak up about homeschooling when the opportunity presents itself, Becky is what I would term an advocate, an active voice in sharing what she has discovered through the opportunity to learn in the company of family, in the rhythm of life.

What does she say to personal friends who are sitting on the fence regarding homeschooling, who are having problems deciding where and with whom their children will spend a major portion of their childhood? "I tell them the kinds of things we're doing, the kinds of things we *can* do. I tell them how much less stress there is in one's life because it doesn't matter *what* the school board decides."

"You can get your laundry done when you're teaching. Put the load in before you start reading with the kids, and change it after you finish reading. I've gone to conferences and spoken with people and answered questions about what it's like being a mother and a teacher also. I had one man ask about my relationship with my husband now that we've been homeschooling. These funny questions people ask, 'What is your relationship with your husband?'"

> **Becky feels that she had a head start over others because she's in a growing yet still small group: second generation homeschoolers.**

"The answer is we're much closer because we're working on something together. He doesn't necessarily teach, but he helps with the laundry. Interestingly, I've found that of the people I'm trying to persuade, the mothers are in favor of it and the husbands are the ones who are against it. Now at least there are some statistics that say the unemployment rate for homeschoolers is very low. Very few homeschoolers have been on unemployment. Now there is something to back up a statement that homeschooling is a feasible option."

Although Becky contemplates her children's life and learning as deeply as any other homeschooling parent, don't think she's the type of mother to just sit around and stress out about her children. Along with homeschooling, she enjoys cooking, skiing, running, biking, reading, playing the piano, and, her "happiest hobby," knitting. "I guess that would be what I consider the greatest gift my parents gave me, an ability and interest in doing a variety of things. The depth and breadth of homeschooling is its most outstanding feature."

Finally, Becky feels that she had a head start over others who turn to homeschooling because she's in a growing yet still small group: second generation homeschoolers.

"First of all I understand what this is, and I know that it works for me so I don't have the same jitters a lot of people have when they're starting out. And," Becky adds, "I have a tremendous resource, two of them actually, at the other end of a phone line."

Kerry Irons, the earliest non-Bangs Wildridge Academy student, went on to earn a master's degree in marine biology. She joins the more than a third of the Academy's 80 students (including all the Bangs children) who obtained a master's, doctoral, or law degree from a major university. "Though we had to name it 'Academy,' it was all homeschooling," Larry concludes. "The process was the same. We had tremendous discussions around the dining room table at lunchtime that would go on and on. There was so much learning happening there."

WHILE I WAS *still in school I had this feeling
that it was stifling me, but I had to take a look
at it from the outside to actually* know *it, to
actually see it.*

15

Keeping a Finger in Many Educational Pies

EDWARD REMBERT

Born: August 25, 1978; Ann Arbor, Michigan
Homeschooling: 1995–1996
Family: Parents—Edward and Venus; Siblings—Isaiah (17), Candace (7)
Most memorable wisdom about life or learning: From parents—Keep your options open; you don't have to follow the set road for anyone.
Favorite study: Early years—Spanish; Middle years—natural sciences, biology; Teen years—science and U.S. history
Current work: Coast Guard Reserve seaman (since 1998); University of Detroit (since 1998), part-time music teacher (since 1997)

Venus literally went by the book and "taught her baby to read" while he was still crawling over reading material. When second child Isaiah came along, she thought the preschool right down the street would be good for 3½-year-old Edward.

"Edward didn't do his work today," his teachers told Venus day after day.

"Was he talking?" she asked.

"No," the teachers would say. "He was quiet."

Holding Edward's little hand on the walk home, Venus asked the boy, "Why didn't you do your work?"

"Well," said Edward, "She wanted us to draw a triangle and color it. One boy went out of the triangle and the teacher was really upset. Mom," he added, "I know what a triangle is."

Indeed he did. Before his baby brother was born, Edward often joined Venus at the high school where she taught math. There, he would climb up on his mom's lap, look at geometric shapes, and ask, "What's that?" Venus would answer, "That's an isosceles triangle. That one is an equilateral triangle." Edward remembered, and even a 3-year-old understands it doesn't make sense to spend a lot of time coloring triangles when you already know all the different kinds.

Would You Like to Take Your Child Home—Please?

Edward's teachers recommended that Venus take him home and teach him math and reading along with his brother. Grandma, also a teacher, was retiring, and stocked the family's bookshelves with her collection. Violin lessons began when Edward was 4, judo lessons when he was 6. Both Edward and Isaiah grew up playing ice hockey.

The boys spent their early years as members of two cultures. Venus' mother is Native American, and the boys spent lots of time on a reservation. "They were quiet kids," remembers Venus, "more introverted, more into nature because of it."

From the reservation, Edward and Isaiah would return to Detroit's black culture. "They spoke differently," Venus says, "and we speak French at home, so the other kids just couldn't understand it. The kids—even those who were kind—would ask the boys, 'Why do you talk different? Why are you like that? Why don't you like this kind of tennis shoes?' It doesn't matter as much now, because those types of things don't matter as you get older."

During what would have been Edward's second-grade year, the Rembert family left Detroit when Edward Sr., needed to attend seminary in a secluded piece of Ohio. A creek flowed in the back property, just beyond the playground. Deer played in the orchard out front, and so did Edward and Isaiah. Another mother with young children suggested the families get together for "very, very loose" lessons, and they would meet in the woods for music or math.

> **Days were filled with climbing trees, library visits, and family performances of Shakespeare's plays.**

Days were filled with climbing trees, library visits, and family performances of Shakespeare's plays. When Venus decided to study music at Ohio Wesleyan University, the boys went, too. "All the students thought they were wonderful," says Venus. "Somebody was always coming to grab them and to let them play drums, tuba, piano, anything."

Eventually, the family returned to Detroit and a ministry for Edward Sr., at his first church. He was also an air force chaplain, which provided plenty of travel opportunities for the family. Edward and Isaiah attended an array of private and alternative schools, including Burton International School, where all who attended (many of the children were from foreign countries) were encouraged to wear traditional dress and "be who they were."

Venus recalls reading that artwork on the walls at home influences the children. When she read this, she immediately took down the living room picture of a storm at sea. It was too late. "Since I was a little guy," says Edward, "I always hung around boats. 'Hey,' I'd holler to people, 'I'll wash your deck for a ride.'"

A High-School Junior Comes Home

Edward was well into his sophomore year of high school when he realized he wasn't really getting all he wanted out of school. His godparents began homeschooling and mentioned it to Edward's parents. Venus was at times disappointed with the private schools the boys attended. "I felt the boys weren't getting enough, academically and more," she explains. "There they were in good schools and I was still doing a lot of the teaching. And I thought if I'm doing a lot of the teaching, I certainly could homeschool. I finally decided we may as well go ahead and do this instead of putting out so much money for all of those schools."

> "I thought maybe I'd miss my friends, maybe I wouldn't have enough to do. You go through a lot of that."

His parents asked Edward if he would like to try homeschooling and he promised to "think about it." While one day faithfully reading the sailing magazine *Cruising World,* he caught an article on homeschooling, then read a few more. The decision whether or not to homeschool wasn't coming easily.

"I had to get used to that idea of not having to get dressed, get out, and go to school. Homeschooling is a different form. It's more free flowing," he says. "I also thought maybe I'd miss my friends, maybe I wouldn't have enough to do. You go through a lot of that,"

Edward reveals. "It turned out that things really picked up. I had more and more to do, but at the beginning I had no way of knowing that would happen."

It took 6 months of weighing the pros and cons—until the middle of his junior year—before Edward chose homeschooling with a bit of reservation. "I figured if I didn't like it I could always go back to school," he says. Brother Isaiah came home at the same time, and friends expressed the wish that their parents would let them come home to learn, too.

The Remberts chose to use Clonlara School's homeschooling program, in part because Edward knew older homeschoolers who had paperwork troubles when they tried to get into college. The homeschoolers *did* get into college but, even knowing this, Edward didn't want to take chances with administrative hassles.

Both Edward and Venus stayed in touch with their Clonlara contact person. Mom helped him review the credits he needed and the possible materials he could use to gain them, then Edward was off on his own learning adventure.

"I'd get up as early as 6 A.M. or as late as 9 A.M., depending on what I had to do that day," he explains. "Clonlara told me what I had to cover and gave me deadlines. Then it was pretty much up to me. That's the thing I like most about homeschooling. There wasn't anybody saying, 'Do this right now.' It was a lot like college. I could get up and study for an hour or two, take off and go for a walk, read a different book, and come back and finish my work. I set my own schedule depending on what I had to get done, and could do it when I felt like it, even if that was late into the night."

Freed from the typical government-school time schedule, the young man found he covered typical schoolwork more easily and rapidly. Freed from the typical government-school methods, Edward discovered another aspect of homeschooling that he liked. "I wasn't just sitting there listening to somebody dictate something, then having to basically regurgitate it back," he enthusiastically shares. "It's active learning; it's not passive. That makes a big difference. I don't like to sit still and learn. I don't like to sit still that much for *anything.* Not that I'm hyperactive," he says, laughing, "but sitting still for hours and hours on end tends to get on my nerves. Especially when you can do the same things with practical applications."

Yes, Edward tells me, "I *was* like that even before homeschooling," but, he adds, "Now I actually know learning *can* be done without sitting still!"

He filled the time free of compulsory school attendance with reading—lots of it. "I read anything," Edwards says. "Textbooks, fiction, love stories, sea stories. You name it, I read it. A lot of magazines, too, like *Cruising World* and *Outdoor Life.*"

All Kinds of Work

Edward got his first job at age 14 as a hockey game scorekeeper for an ice arena and has worked whenever he has wanted to since. At the local A&W, he entertained as the A&W Bear. After 2 years of very hot summers in his bearskin, he switched to washing dishes and delivering food for a riverfront café where the cook insisted Edward learn how to use the kitchen while he was there.

Volunteering all summer long at a camp for underprivileged children gave the young man first-hand experience dealing with huge amounts of childhood energy while he held down responsibility for an entire class. Edward gave more volunteer time to a House the Homeless project, as well as to activities sponsored by his church.

A passion for old western movies united with an interest in U.S. history led Edward to visit historical reenactments from time to time, always wishing he could participate. In 1995, shortly after he had begun his homeschooling journey and realized he had more time to call his own, a parade came to town, and in it proudly rode the

Buffalo Soldiers, representatives of America's black cavalry from 1865 until World War II.

"Hey," Edward hollered as they rode past. "How can I join your group?"

"If you're really serious about it," a soldier answered from atop his horse, "meet us back at the stables at the end of the parade." Edward walked to the stables where he learned that the Buffalo Soldiers commit to monthly organizational meetings along with whatever preparation is necessary to answer calls to come speak at schools, appear at benefits and parades, and, the fun part, reenact battles. He signed up on the spot.

Often, the group—25 to 30 members strong—gathers for a full weekend of camping in their expensive replica uniforms. A favorite is Michigan's Crossroads Village, a replica of an 1870 town with a train running through it. Reenactments of full-blown cavalry charges require "really big, open spaces" and send Edward packing to Illinois or Ohio.

Just one group on a list of reenactors around the nation, the Buffalo Soldiers received a call one day. "We need four men between the ages of 18 and 40, between 5' 6" and 5' 7" tall," said the voice on the other end of the phone. Production of the movie *The Rough Riders*, starring Tom Berringer and Sam Elliot, was about to begin. Historically, Buffalo soldiers were relatively small and lightweight, so the horses could carry the men quickly for long distances. The movie production company was looking for extras who could maintain historical accuracy.

> He filled the time free of compulsory school attendance with reading —lots of it. "I read anything," Edwards says.

Edward's flexible schedule allowed him to leave home for the estimated month-long adventure. His fellow Buffalo Soldiers made sure he brought books to study, and they flew to Texas to become part of a movie cast.

"We shot in two locations," says Edward, "and stayed about 5 weeks. I didn't really miss home; I was too busy in a totally different world. They pay you to be ready, and we usually had to be on the set at 5 A.M. One morning we got there at 8 A.M. only to wait around until 10 at night. Then we did the scene at least 20 times."

In case you're inclined to rent the video and watch for him, Edward appears in the second half of *The Rough Riders*. "The best place to see me is just before the charge of San Juan Hill," he says. "The camera looks down a line of soldiers, and there you will see my face." He would enjoy being a movie extra again, but experience proved the job of movie star isn't nearly as glamorous as people make it out to be.

With Clonlara's diploma tucked under his belt, Edward now keeps a finger in many educational pies by combining part-time endeavors. For 3 years, he's been self-employed as a private violin teacher for several students. Sometimes he substitute teaches at the Waldorf school where Venus is a teacher and his home-schooling little sister, Candace, attends classes 3 half-days each week.

> **With Clonlara's diploma tucked under his belt, Edward now keeps a finger in many educational pies by combining part-time endeavors.**

Edward is also a part-time student at the University of Detroit, 2 years into "academic exploration" to discover what he truly likes. He'll need to choose a major before hitting his junior year; today he's leaning toward a move into teaching, quite possibly in the Waldorf method, which he compares favorably to homeschooling. "They emphasize being creative and not setting a mold for all children," he explains. "My interest has been piqued by spending lots of time at the school, watching the staff, watching the children with the staff." He figures he should have his degree in 2 to 3 years.

Part time is key to his third job, too, as a seaman in the U.S. Coast Guard Reserves. It's not really a surprise choice of military service for a young man who's had an affinity for water since he was a child. For the past 2 years, Edward has given them one weekend a month. He calls the Coast Guard "a tad bit more humanitarian than the other branches of service. You're out there to save people, and I liked that. I'm learning more and more about boating, and it's possible I'll request a station change in order to get to travel a bit while being paid for it."

The seaman doubts he'll take the option of joining the Coast Guard full time. If things go the way I plan, says Edward, "I intend to sail around the world." (Yes, I've attempted to hook up Edward with a hero of his—Robin Lee Graham, the homeschooler of chapter 11. Boy, did Edward get a kick out of knowing they would be in a book together!) He may sail around the world in a 26-foot sailboat acquired through one of those "once-in-a-lifetime opportunities" that happen too many times in too many homeschooled children's lives to any longer consider these occurrences mere coincidence.

> **"Once-in-a-lifetime opportunities" happen too many times in too many homeschooled children's lives to any longer consider these occurrences mere coincidence.**

One day, as a boy named Josh finished up his music lesson with Venus, his father, Joe, came to pick him up. Joe announced he was going sailing. "Edward talked to us about sailing and boats every day," explains Venus. "We'd all look at each other and say, 'Uh-oh, here we go again!' I told Joe about Edward's passion."

"I'd be happy to take him out," said Joe. "Did you know I teach sailing courses?"

Edward and Isaiah learned to sail with Joe on the waters of Lake St. Claire, Lake Erie, and Lake Huron. In the process, they all became friends.

On a bittersweet afternoon, Josh's mom came to pick him up from lessons. She told the Remberts that a friend of Joe's was dying of cancer and wanted Joe to have his impressive sailboat. Joe, in turn, wanted his own boat to go "to somebody in the family." Since Edward and Isaiah had become like sons to him, Joe sold the boat to the brothers for one-third of its value. They spent this past summer sailing and trying in vain to get Venus out on a moonlight cruise.

What's the pattern repeated in homeschoolers' lives that I mentioned? The once-in-a-lifetime opportunity knocking for so many homeschoolers?

(1) By living and learning together, parent is well aware of child's passion.

(2) Parent and child either create or leap on every opportunity to pursue that passion; opportunity often appears in the form of a mentor.

(3) Child and mentor develop mutual respect, friendship, and an adult-adult relationship.

(4) Mentor offers what he or she can to help the child along his or her path, sometimes in unexpected ways.

Now a black belt, Edward calls judo another favorite hobby. In his dwindling spare time, he still engages in reenactment activities.

Someday, Edward would like to raise a family and thinks homeschooling his children—at least during part of their childhood—is in the cards. Here, the values instilled in him may extend into another generation. "From the beginning my parents taught us right from wrong," he says. "By the time I got to be 14, they said, 'You know what you should or shouldn't do, and we trust you to do that. Everybody's going to make mistakes; just be careful.' I felt their trust," Edward adds. "They're really supportive."

His definition of a successful life is among the briefest in this book. "It's one where you're happy. That's the in and out of it. If you're happy doing what you're doing, then that would be it."

I DON'T KNOW *where she got the idea, but Mom started hanging up cool sayings on the bathroom wall as we grew up and learned to read, constantly adding them as she found them. They said things like: Mistakes show us what needs improving, mistakes are the portals of discovery; Don't let what you're being get in the way of what you might become; and one from Albert Schweitzer—"One thing I know. The only ones among you who will be really happy are those who will have sought and found how to serve." Those were phrases and sayings that meant a lot to me.*

16

Passion-Filled Learning Ignites a Career

CHUCK DOBSON

Age: 21; born Fredericksburg, Virginia

Homeschooling: 1985–1997

Family: Parents—Gary and Linda; Siblings—Erika (19), Adam (16)

Most memorable wisdom about life or learning: It really doesn't matter what others are doing or learning; I'm the best judge of knowing what I need and where I should be regarding my own education.

Favorite study: Early years—learning to read; Middle years—social studies, social science, history (mostly U.S.); Teen years—fire fighting and emergency medical services

Current work: Fire driver; Tupper Lake (NY) Fire Department (since 1999); emergency services technician, Adirondack Medical Center emergency room (since 1997)

Here's an adult homeschooler whose story I know as well as my own. As the one who decided in 1985 to take back the responsibility for his education and bring it home, over the years I have shared a lot with my son. It seems only fitting that we should also share this chapter.

Little Mr. Happy-Go-Lucky's Disappearing Act

With an October birthday, Chuck slipped past the compulsory school attendance age net for almost a full extra year before the law demanded he leave home, or at least so I thought. At the time I had never heard of homeschooling, so with a heavy heart I registered him for kindergarten. Gosh, did he look tiny as he lifted first one, then another short leg to climb the steep steps of the school bus. I wondered if all, or even most, moms felt as empty as I did watching the bus drive away. More important—if they did feel this way—why did everybody do it anyway?

> I wondered if most moms felt as empty as I did watching the bus drive away. More important—if they *did* feel this way—why did everybody do it anyway?

The school originally scheduled Chuck to attend afternoon kindergarten. I called and told whoever was in charge of schedules that I had observed Chuck was a morning person, and it would be much better if he was placed in a morning class. (At the time I didn't know a parent wasn't supposed to do things like this. I had also thought the teacher would more likely be in a better frame of mind with the morning class, but chose not to mention this on the phone.) *Only* because a bus happened to be going by our home at the right time was my request accommodated.

This meant that instead of riding home from school with the older kids, Chuck was with them on the way *to* school. It took only until the weather got cold enough for the older kids to write things in the frost on the bus windows. Curious, Chuck began asking what curse words meant. My husband Gary and I thought, "Now there's a lesson we really didn't want him to have." Was he getting others?

The first two report cards Chuck brought home, teeming with S's for "satisfactory" and I's for "needs improvement" in a gazillion categories, bore the news that he didn't know half the things I knew he knew when he took that giant step on to the bus. (After all, he'd watched Sesame Street in the ol' days when they told us it was good for children, shortly before they told us it was bad for children.)

Chuck also talked a lot in class, which was *not* news to Little Mr. Happy-Go-Lucky's mom. "Oh, how nice, he's a good communicator," I thought to myself despite the "I" under behavior. I've always been rather shy, so it was with great amazement and a pinch of pride that I watched my baby grow into a gregarious little boy.

I'd always figured it was a combination of the teacher telling him to be quiet and the fellow kindergartner who bullied him every day on the bus ride home that turned Little Mr. Happy-Go-Lucky into a stressed-out and an all of a sudden not-very-fun-to-be-around guy. Fortunately, his little sister doesn't remember this time, as she became Chuck's short-cut to frustration release.

"School is like an assembly line type of thing, you know," Chuck tells me as we talk at the kitchen table after a tour of the house he has just moved into. "There were a lot of kindergartners. The teacher didn't really care about any of us."

"You noticed that while you there?" I try to hide the shock.

"Sure. I can also remember feeling inferior. It wasn't unbearable. I just didn't feel comfortable a lot of the time." (The things you learn when you write a book.)

Back then, I did know that we were losing Little Mr. Happy-Go-Lucky. I started going to the classroom as often as I could, which wasn't a lot with a toddler and newborn at home. Chuck didn't look happy there; in fact, none of the kids looked overjoyed to be there. "It was like a job," Chuck remembers. "It was something I had to do."

Early in the second half of the kindergarten year the telephone rang. It was the school principal, the same person who had just gone down to Chuck's classroom, yanked him out of class, and asked him if he'd written the filthy note he'd passed along to a girl in his class.

"No," Chuck told the principal. "One of the boys on the bus asked me to give it to her so I did."

The principal didn't seem to believe Chuck. I did. (As brilliant as he was he couldn't have put that letter together at the time.) I was stunned. I was insulted. I was angry with myself that this principal, a person whom neither Chuck nor I really knew and would never have known under any other circumstances, held so much sway over my son's life and how he would be perceived in that school from that moment forward.

> **John Holt said I didn't *have* to send Chuck to school, that he could learn at home. (He didn't actually say Chuck, but that's what I heard.)**

You may (or may not) remember the *Phil Donahue Show*, a popular talk show in the eighties when the few that existed actually sometimes exposed viewers to stimulating conversation. I wasn't a regular viewer, but I turned it on one morning shortly after the "filthy note incident." Phil Donahue's guest was John Holt, who "would be right back to talk about homeschooling."

What a morning! John said I didn't *have* to send Chuck to school, that he could learn at home. (He didn't actually say Chuck, but that's what I heard.) John said others were doing so quite successfully. John said it was often better for kids who were having all kinds of different problems in school. FLASH! BANG! The idea just *felt* so right. I loved Chuck. I could get him through reading, writing, and arithmetic, and we could worry about tomorrow tomorrow.

We were living in the New Jersey suburbs at the time, surrounded by malls and the steadily increasing traffic stream from the growing industrial park nearby. To make a long story short, we moved to the mountains—far away from the shopping Mecca and the annoying sound of traffic 100 feet from the front door. We pulled Chuck out of first grade, which he had only attended for 2 weeks, and started a new life, one that included homeschooling our children. The little boy, it turns out, understood well that his parents were upset with the government school system.

Mr. Happy-Go-Lucky Returns

We had been in our new home about a month when it started to snow . . . and snow . . . and snow. I'd never even *imagined* that much snow in my worst nightmares. Our closest neighbors weren't very close, and we knew nobody. I had no idea what the state laws were about homeschooling and, I guess, didn't care, so I didn't report the recent presence of a school-aged child to anybody. The boys' new bedroom was huge, so one side became our home schoolroom, complete with bookcases brimming with books, paper, and crayons, a child-size table and chairs, and the laminated, perfectly printed a-b-c strip Chuck brought home when kindergarten ended.

"I still didn't like typical schoolwork," recalls Chuck, "not for a while. I liked learning to read, though. That was fun. That's probably why I got more interested in schoolwork after a while, after learning to read."

For the first few months, we used the fun and painless Ball-Stick-Bird series to learn how to read. Chuck didn't know it, but I believe there was another reason he eventually learned to appreciate learning more; mom's subscription to *Home Education*

Magazine. Thanks to its constant food for thought in this area, homeschooling eventually evolved from school-at-home to something else; something more fun, more active, more meaningful, more in line with the way Chuck was wired to learn. I learned to observe and trust the signals Chuck gave me. The signals never led toward textbooks and stupendous academic achievement. Instead, they signaled a detour toward giving Chuck's gregarious nature free rein.

The years filled with activity as the children grew, and we eventually became "legal" homeschoolers. "I socialized with same-aged peers through Boy Scouts, going to the park for skating and basketball. I joined Little League, swim classes, had sleep-overs, and went to school dances," says Chuck.

> **The signals never led toward textbooks and stupendous academic achievement. Instead, they signaled a detour toward giving Chuck's gregarious nature free rein.**

After a few years, the state-supported Visitors' Interpretative Center (VIC), a nature center showcasing our little piece of the Adirondack Park, opened only a short 10-minute drive away. It appeared to be a real "socialization opportunity" when the only other thing a short 10-minute drive away was a general store. "We visited the VIC a lot and took Junior Naturalist classes there, so I learned quite a bit about nature and the outdoors," says Chuck. "I wanted to learn more, so when I was 12 I spoke to someone about volunteering. As a volunteer I led nature trail walks for school students and the public, made slide presentations, watched the information desk and gave out information to the public, and gave tours of the exhibits. At first I volunteered about 8 hours each week, but as I got older it escalated closer to 16 hours a week." Chuck adds, "I've always been friends with people of all ages, including a lot of adults. I got to know many of the senior citizens at the VIC who also volunteered."

Mr. Happy-Go-Lucky was definitely back and blooming, doing what he loved and loving what he did. Chuck's learning storehouse increased with each visit to the VIC. "One of my mentors at that time, a naturalist named Mike Storey, is very knowledgeable and a very nice man," Chuck explains. "He took me under his wing for a long time. I really enjoyed that work." The staff and volunteers were helping me educate my son and, right along with me, enjoying watching him blossom into a young man.

When 14 year-old Chuck's grandparents visited for a few summer days, we spent a lot of time wandering around town. Passersby greeted Chuck, truck horns honked to elicit his wave, and store clerks asked him how he was doing. On the evening of my folks' last night with us we stood in line waiting for a table at a restaurant. Chuck excused himself momentarily and walked over to the restaurant's largest table around which sat ten or so senior citizens. "Hello, Chuckie!" filled the air.

"Martha, I thought you were still in Europe," Chuck returned. "Thanks for the postcard from Italy. Hal, I hope you're going to be there to help me with the tour group Friday. Good to see you—enjoy your dinner!"

"Geez," Dad said, "this whole visit has been like going around town with the mayor!" (Indeed, when I recently ran for election to town council, I seriously considered creating campaign literature that said only, "Vote for Chuckie's Mom.")

Chuck pegs this period as the time he took charge of his own education. New York State homeschooling regulations require quarterly reports on activity, and since it was *his* education, I turned responsibility for these over to Chuck. "I felt very in charge then," he says. "I knew I could get as much accomplished as I wanted. I studied many of the typical high school subjects, often with alternative material. I coordinated what I wanted to study with Mom, set goals, and met those goals, and the rest of the time was available to explore different subjects or do something else I wanted to do."

Passion Ignites

That "something else" also came along when Chuck was 14. He joined the Boy Scouts Explorer post for fire fighting. "I signed up because my friend, the man next door, was putting the post together," Chuck explains. "The post is designed for young people to learn about a profession until they're old enough to, in this case, fight fires. A lot of people ask me how much time I put into it, but I could never put a number on it. There were two meetings and a training each month. We also had an average of four fire calls and two activities each month, activities being work details, extra meetings, state training, drills, fire prevention open house, and a lot of community programs, too."

> At 16, the homeschooler was employed by the state, had his own health insurance, and was socking away retirement funds.

Chuck fails to mention that many fire and rescue calls come in the middle of the night, and for well over 2 years he couldn't get himself to the firehouse. I graciously allowed Chuck's father to participate in our family's "after midnight homeschooling" by becoming chief taxi driver. Chuck was happy with this arrangement, especially after one particularly frigid midnight run with me. On taking the first turn off our street, my unwarmed-up car died and refused to take us any farther. Chuck hitched a ride to the firehouse with a passing fire fighter. In the dark, and wearing only pajamas under winter coat and boots, I walked home. Our neighbor, the one who started the Explorer post, finally told Chuck that if he could be ready and standing in his driveway when he, too, left for calls, Chuck wouldn't have to wake his parents. I don't think the kid ever missed a call.

Itching for independent transportation, Chuck knew he needed a job to support a car. He didn't have to look far. The manager of the gift shop inside the VIC happily employed Chuck until a job with more hours opened up with the VIC itself. At 16, the home-schooler was employed by the state, had his own health insurance, and was socking away retirement funds.

The local community college donates a few credit hours to the VIC to be given to a volunteer and, when he was 16, the credits were presented to Chuck. "I used that certificate to take an environmental science course," he says. "It gave me a lot of information to take back to my volunteer job. It also allowed me to put together many of the things I'd already learned and get a clearer understanding of it from a scientific standpoint. It was nice of the VIC to do that for me, and they got something back, too."

This was the beginning of Chuck's transition toward a more traditional educational route. The transition happened so smoothly we never really noticed an end to homeschooling and a beginning of "something else." Looking back, it just seems like a natural progression for the maturing son who had so often independently pursued his interests. Chuck has leisurely taken more courses since then.

With 3 years of training and answering calls under his belt, Chuck turned 17, and came to dinner one night to state what I knew by this time was inevitable: He wanted to become a full-fledged member of the volunteer fire department. Due to his age, he needed parental permission.

"I've known for 2 years this is what I want to do, Mom," he said. Previously demonstrated dedication and the conviction in his voice allowed me to swallow the speech I'd prepared about the dangers involved and to sign the permission form. With a majority vote of the fire department membership, Chuck became its newest and youngest fire fighter. The next paper he brought home was a $100,000 life insurance policy in case he was killed in duty.

What does Chuck see as homeschooling's role in all of this? "More time," he states. "More time to put towards my interests, more time to spend learning what I wanted to learn. By the time I became an actual fire fighter," he continues, "I was ready to help teach the basic course. Every time the instructor would do a tactical rotation he'd have me man one of the stations. Having spent 3 years training already, I was beyond elementary knowledge."

While attending rescue calls as a fireman, Chuck observed the work of EMTs (emergency medical technicians) and noticed that they didn't always have as much qualified help as they could have used. At age 17, while taking every New York State fire-fighting course within 100 miles of home, Chuck studied for 6 months, became an EMT, and volunteered with the local rescue squad. The training then led to a job with the Olympic venues in Lake Placid, New York, where he collected far too many addresses and phone numbers from female skaters.

At 19 years old, he became the fire department's safety training officer, finished second level EMT training, and jumped into a rare job opening as a hospital emergency services tech. But Chuck had long harbored the dream of becoming a paid fire fighter. He left the emergency room after a 12-hour shift early one morning, took the Civil Service test (which was required for fire fighting employment), and made the highest score.

A position in another town opened up within weeks, and suddenly Chuck's dream came true. Of course, this meant leaving a department and friends he'd worked with for 7 years. "I'm still dealing with the changes," Chuck says. "I'm a little homesick, but the upside is obvious."

He considers himself fortunate that homeschooling allowed him to discover work—possibly life's work—that he loves. "Mom always told us to do what we love, that the money would follow, and then her writing became a real-life example of that," Chuck says. "Even though the odds were slim of finding a paying job, when practically all fire fighting is voluntary, Mom's 'main homeschooling lesson' kept me going."

Always an active guy, Chuck remains resentful that as a New York homeschooler he couldn't play interscholastic baseball and football. Still, he'd choose the homeschooling way of life again. "My socialization with other kids my age exposed me to their talk about what their days were like and what school was like," Chuck says. "I know I had it good in comparison. Looking back it was a good thing, a positive thing," he adds, "even when I was kind of skeptical about it. I can't really compare homeschooling to public schooling because I didn't experience their way. I do know that if I'm interested in something I can research it better than a lot of people I know."

> **"My socialization with other kids my age exposed me to their talk about what their days were like and what school was like. I know I had it good in comparison."**

Chuck says he felt "a bit socially isolated" during early high school years, but with so much going on "I didn't really have time to care." He feels homeschooling interfered with meeting girls "somewhat," but adds that this was probably beneficial since "I was focusing my energy on learning rather than on trying to get a date." When there were dates, though, the topic of homeschooling did emerge, and reaction for the most part was positive. "They'd either say they'd never heard of it, or say they knew someone else doing it," Chuck explains. "The latter is a reaction that happens more now, though."

The young man admits, "I don't know much about child psychology or raising children," but speaking from his own experience he feels "a child's most impressionable time is when he's young. That's when homeschooling is most important. After all," he says, "who would you rather have decide how a child's going to be—you, or other little kids and teachers?"

While he'd like to have children one day, he wonders if it will be financially feasible for a potential spouse to stay home and do so. Indeed, I'd already pointed out "you'll never be 'rich' in this line of work," and asked what compensates for that.

"I get to do what I like to do and get paid *something* for it," Chuck answers.

It all fits neatly into his brief definition of a successful life. "A job that makes you happy," Chuck begins. "Being with someone who makes you happy—or being by yourself if that makes you happy. That's it—being happy doing what you want to do."

The future may hold continued work in fire fighting, or possibly a shift into police work. "Investigation is what I'd like to do eventually. It's like solving puzzles," says the young man who grew up doing plenty of that.

Homeschooling's Impact on Parents

"What impact did homeschooling have on your parents?" is a question asked of all our adult homeschoolers. When presented with this question, Chuck answers, "Mom stayed home and didn't work, so Dad had to work a little more and was gone more often. We stretched money a little more, but I think Mom was pretty happy staying home with us."

Oh, boy, was I. The impact of homeschooling, however, went much deeper than the blessing of enjoying life and learning with my children. Other homeschooling parents in this book reported what I felt as well: that the act of taking responsibility for our children's education made an indelible change.

That change is most often an internal one. Almost unanimously, the parents in this book pointed to a powerful shift in their thinking about schooling as an unquestioningly accepted societal institution. As Georgia Taylor and Edward Rembert point out in their chapters, you can't see the *real* workings of a system until you are no longer part of it. (This is also why it's so much easier for humans to note what's wrong with others than it is to note what's wrong with ourselves.)

Many of the homeschooling parents spent a little or a lot of time researching institutional educational practices, then compared the philosophies behind the practices with events unfolding under their own roof. Many routinely accepted school practices seemed unnecessary or even antithetical to learning, raising even more questions and concerns. Some parents emerged with the very real feeling they had been deceived in their own schooling. Others questioned that if their parental instincts were screaming the antithesis of what educational experts espouse, could experts in other arenas be equally wrong? If anyone will find out, it will be a homeschooling parent.

> Almost unanimously, the parents represented in this book pointed to a powerful shift in their thinking about schooling as an unquestioningly accepted societal institution.

As in the full range of society, home-schooling parents' minds seem to open to the degree they are willing to research, step away, and try something different *despite* what others may think or say. In so doing, they aren't exactly choosing the easiest way to travel through life, but they find the difficulties are miniscule compared to what they and their children could lose if they don't apply the knowledge they possess to raising their children.

As I hope the people in this book demonstrate to you, the lion's share of homeschooled children don't suffer academically, nor do they become societal burdens on welfare rolls or in jails. On the contrary, they emerge as intelligent, confident, responsible adults who overwhelmingly define life success in terms of love and happiness, and look forward to a continuing learning lifestyle in a world of infinite possibility.

Even today in her little town this shy writer encounters folks she's never spoken with before. "Are you Chuckie's mom?" is almost always the question that follows my introduction.

"Yes, I am," I answer. I've learned to anticipate the wonderful comments that are music to a homeschooling parent's ear. As tempting as it may be to claim credit for myself, I discovered many moons ago that the tribute these kind words convey belongs to home-schooling and the benefits it confers by emancipating children from compulsory school attendance.

Let educational freedom ring.

2

The Younger Set

17
Night Owl

MELISSA SCONYERS

Born: March 16, 1984; Los Angeles, California

Homeschooling: 1996 to present

Family: Parents—Hugh and Sima; Siblings—Stephanie (16), Justin (11)

Most memorable wisdom about life or learning: From parents—You can't wait around for somebody to teach it to you. Just go and do it yourself.

Favorite study: Early years—writing and reading ("I can't remember not being able to read"); Middle years—English, computers; Teen years— English, computers, public speaking, sports

Current work: Self-employed, Web and graphic design (since 1994)

Life began for Melissa in Los Angeles' Cedar Sinai Hotel. "It's where all the famous people are born," says the 15-year-old, newly in possession of a driver's permit at the beginning of our time together. We had an appointment to talk; Melissa received my call on a cell phone outside of a movie matinee that she was attending with friends, after lunch with friends, which had followed a soccer game with friends.

Mom Sima, a doctor easing her way out of work as medical director of an HMO (health maintenance organization), wasn't totally prepared for what would happen after she inadvertently planted the seed of homeschooling in Melissa's mind. The family had just left California, where Melissa had attended private school, for Austin, Texas. There, Hugh and Sima made sure to buy a house in a good school district for their three young children. But Texas has what Sima calls "Robin Hood taxation." School districts with more money are forced to give away money to school districts with less. "I soon got involved on the board of a foundation to raise money for our school district," says Sima.

It was on the Internet that Sima discovered the concept of homeschooling, but it piqued her interest at first for different reasons than those of most parents. "If a school district could provide classroom space and a teacher for homeschoolers," she says, "then in some states those homeschoolers, even though they were loosely—very, very loosely—affiliated with the school district, could still be counted by the school district as heads."

"To get the money?" I ask.

"Right. I thought that would be very useful in our school district," Sima continues, "because we needed the heads but we had no room for the bodies. To find out more, I did a *lot* of research on homeschooling."

All year, Melissa had been experiencing an "insolvable problem" with the teacher of "her most favorite thing in life"—English. The teacher made belittling, ridiculing comments to Melissa, and persisted in doing so even after Melissa explained to her how much the remarks hurt her feelings. Toward the end of this disappointing seventh-grade school year, she asked if she could stay home from "sport's day."

"I'm not going to learn anything," Melissa told her mom. "It's going to be the popular kids being picked."

"All that usual stuff," adds Sima, who told her daughter she could stay home.

"Great!" cheered Melissa. "I can go out and roller-blade."

"Oh, no, you can't just be out on the street," Sima cautioned her. "There's a law that kids are supposed to be in school during school hours unless they're homeschooling."

"What's homeschooling?" Melissa asked.

Sima gave a brief sketch. The girl who had complained about boredom in some classes and being lost in others immediately caught on to the benefits of the concept.

"You can go at your own pace when you know something. You can buzz forward or take as long as you need!" she exclaimed.

With just a few weeks left in the school year, both mother and daughter contemplated the advantages and disadvantages of homeschooling, "There was another incident with the English teacher that was horrendous," Sima says.

> The girl who had complained about boredom in some classes and being lost in others immediately caught on to the benefits of the concept.

One of the teacher's favored students asked Melissa for an answer during a test. Melissa was caught talking when she answered "I don't know, and even if I did I wouldn't tell you." The teacher threw so many accusations and abusive remarks at Melissa that the girl who was trying to cheat confessed, saying, "Melissa wasn't cheating. I asked her a question and she didn't give me the answer." The teacher continued her torment through the next class period while Melissa's classmates went to lunch.

"That was it," says Sima. "Melissa just said, 'I'm done. I'm not going back.'"

So how does a young gal, intuitively enamored by home-schooling as a solution to school problems, go about her day? Well, often at night.

"That's when I do my best work—and all of my Web site work," Melissa says. "I think my most productive hours are between 11 P.M. and 4 A.M."

This may be when Melissa attends to her current Web and graphic design business, one in a long line of businesses she's created since she was 10 years old. ("I sold seashells in the park when I was 2.") But she also practices speed skating five times a week, competing about once a month. She's the youngest member of Women in Technology International (WITI) and met her mentors by regularly attending meetings. She plans to get back into horseback riding and start a vault team (performing gymnastics on horseback). The Sconyers' family nanny, a college student named Felicia, has been introducing Melissa and her siblings to lots of new places around Austin and teaching her how to drive. Along with this long list of activities, Melissa plays soccer with a homeschool team and loves photography and art.

> "Sometimes I'll get really inspired to work on a Web site for 18 hours straight. I wouldn't be able to do that if I wasn't homeschooling."

With homeschooler Makonnen David Blake Hannah (see chapter 25), Melissa designed eBiz 4 Teens, the award-winning Web site created as a ThinkQuest entry. ThinkQuest is an international educational initiative committed to advancing learning through the use of computer and networking technology in a collaborative manner. While in California for the awards ceremony, Melissa got the chance to give an impromptu presentation about the Web site and ran well over the 15-minute time limit.

"There are two types of homeschooling, in my opinion," Melissa says. "They are school at home and homeschooling. School at home is basically just bringing school to home. That's not how I work. Sometimes I don't do math for a week, and then sometimes I'll do math *all* week! It just depends on what I feel like doing. Sometimes I'll get really inspired to work on a Web site for 18 hours straight. I wouldn't be able to do that if I wasn't homeschooling."

Melissa remembers one more thing she likes about homeschooling—her collection of work clothes. "I usually never take off my pajamas," she says. "I have more pajamas than anything else."

18

Writing Fever

MATT WORSHAM

Born: October 3, 1985; Dallas, Texas

Homeschooling: 1993 to present

Family: Parents—Ronald and Anne; Siblings—Daniel (12), Whitney (9), Hayley (5)

Most memorable wisdom about life or learning: Parents—The harder it is the more you get. Work hard and keep at what you're doing. Play with your talents.

Favorite study: Early years—science, anything in astronomy; Middle years—same

Current work: Columnist, *Daily Herald* (Provo, Utah, since 1999)

Matt was bored and academically ahead of his classmates in his public school in Orem, Utah. Mom Anne knew he couldn't stand being there. A few weeks into his third-grade attendance, she "sort of tossed out the idea of homeschooling."

Matt's reaction startled Anne. He fell to his knees. "Please, oh, please, Mom," he begged. "Let's homeschool."

It wasn't too difficult a decision for a mother who taught him to read by letting him crawl to the proper flash card. The precocious little boy didn't start conversing until he was 4 years old, then launched immediately into questions such as, "Dad, what does tertiary mean?"

Homeschooling sounded like so much fun that younger sisters Whitney and Hayley asked to be homeschooled, too. Whitney came home for first grade, then in third grade returned to government school. "It's a social thing," Anne whispers. Younger brother Daniel, autistic and developmentally delayed, attends special programs in the school system.

The homeschooling day begins for Matt around 6 A.M. After a quick shower and breakfast, Matt's ready for the books at 7 A.M. "I use a Saxon [publisher] math book," he says, "and other books I choose from the library or some Mom buys at the bookstore. Math takes up about half of my time, then all the other typical subjects are mostly reading and a little bit of writing. I especially like to read fiction," he adds. "The Harry Potter books are very good."

Matt figures he's about "70 percent in charge" of his own education. "Mom sets down standards, and she won't let me give up science or math completely," he explains. "I control other things I want to do, and how fast or slow I go."

Anne quickly interjects—not the first time she speaks to Matt directly. "A lot of times, you can figure out which science you want to study or what you want to write. The only thing I'm really determined about is math," she says, with a laugh. "But you have a lot of freedom in other things, like computers, Visual Basic [a computer language], writing, reading, science."

By lunchtime, most bookwork is out of the way. When friends return home from school around 2:30, Matt catches up with them in the neighborhood, at Boy Scout meetings and activities, or at church. He's back home in time for dinner, followed by family read-alouds and philosophical discussions.

So what about all that free afternoon time? Even though Matt didn't like to write when he was going to school, once he came home it became a passion. He and Anne are collaborating on a children's fiction book, tentatively titled *The Case of the Poisonous Polluters.* If it's anywhere close to deadline time, Matt works on his newspaper column about the Internet for kids, circulated every Sunday to 35,000 people via the *Daily Herald* of Provo, Utah.

The newspaper's editor, who offered then 13-year-old Matt the job, lured the columnist and article writer with 2 years' experience away from the *Utah County Journal.* Anne used to pay Matt $5 per piece for the *Journal* since the newspaper didn't compensate him. Today, the *Daily Herald* keeps him on their payroll at $20 per column.

> **The newspaper's editor who offered then 13-year-old Matt the job lured a columnist and article writer with 2 years' experience away from *The Utah County Journal.***

Matt's first column for the *Journal* was a combination of humor and information and brought opportunities to interview a former Miss America, a Nobel Prize winner, the Brigham Young University football coach, and Richard Paul Evan, author of *The Christmas Box.* Matt's hands-down favorite interview was with Larry King.

Acting in her unofficial capacity as Matt's public relations secretary, Anne says, "When I set up the appointment, I forgot to mention to Larry King's secretary that Matt was 11 years old. It was a hush-hush meeting, top secret. We were put into the 'secret room,' then Larry King was ushered in, accompanied by a security agent, to meet with the reporter who would interview him."

There sat Matt with his trusty tape recorder. "Larry King was wonderful," says Anne. "He shook hands with Matt, then with his sisters, while asking their names. He took it totally seriously. Later, when I shared the finished article with King, he said, 'Yeah, I remember him; that was a great kid!'"

Anne, a newspaper reporter herself, tried a brief stint at full-time work while homeschooling, but it lasted only 3 months. Four months after the *Daily Herald* hired Matt, he jokes that he got his mom a part-time job there, too.

Matt found his second passion around the same time. "If I'm not playing with my friends and I'm not reading, I'm on the computer," he says. Matt's proud of his best-in-the-neighborhood computer, and the speedy DSL (digital subscriber line) he talked dad Ronald, a Brigham Young University accounting professor, into getting.

"My impossible dream is to be syndicated and be a millionaire by 16," he jokes as I ask him what the future holds. "Actually," he says, "I'm torn between several options. I could go into a career in computers; that would be good for me. I could become a writer; that would also be fun. I could become a professor of computers or writing, or become a computer writer. If I can have what I want, I'll combine computers and writing somehow."

There *are* a couple of things Matt doesn't like about homeschooling. "Home-cooked lunches is one," he giggles, as Anne admits that their lunches are "a little bad." And when he's sick, he still has to work, he complains.

Homeschooling contributes to Matt's view of a successful life being one in which a person is happy following a passion. "My creativity is much wider than it would be in public school," he says. "Homeschooling let me break out of the mold. Now teachers aren't shaping my future—I am. I'm taking control of my own destiny, my own path."

19

A Propensity for Solitude

RIKKI SCANDORA

Born: July 19, 1984; Bellevue, Washington
Homeschooling: 1991 to present
Family: Parents—Keith and Julie; Siblings: Rhiannon (17), Ty (12)
Most memorable wisdom about life or learning: Mentor—Forget that you're trying to learn something and just let it happen.
Favorite Study: Early years—can't recall specific goals; Middle years—increasingly interested in animals and outdoors, art somewhat; Teen years—even more interest in animals, outdoors, nature
Current work: Homeschooling student

When Keith and Julie Scandora were married, they both planned to continue in their management jobs with a telephone company. Julie took off the maximum time allowed with the birth of each child, but soon the couple sent each offspring into full-time day care.

As daughters Rhiannon and Rikki grew to compulsory school attendance age, Keith and Julie researched and took advantage of Washington State's wide array of educational options in the form of alternative school attendance for their girls. All, however, was not well.

> **The ideas inherent in homeschooling would require a 180-degree turn in philosophy for a mom who originally thought homeschooling "a horrible idea."**

Rikki knows why she came home in the middle of second grade. A year before, Julie turned to the public library for help in deciding how her children should be educated. First she read Charles Silberman's *Crisis in the Classroom,* then stumbled upon *How Children Learn* by John Holt. The ideas inherent in homeschooling, laid out by Holt, appeared to be a solution but would require a 180-degree turn in philosophy for a mom who originally thought homeschooling "a horrible idea."

"My parents saw a change in me after kindergarten," explains Rikki. "I was being forced to learn and quickly turning away from *wanting* to learn. By the end of the year, I wouldn't complete the journaling I loved at the beginning of the year. I was becoming very depressed with school."

Julie recalls a young Rikki as energetic and strong willed—"the perfect candidate for homeschooling so these traits wouldn't be totally lost." Like other homeschooled children, Rikki is also highly self-aware. Without peer influence shaping or overshadowing her personality, she has recognized and accepted her character traits. "I'm happy *not* being around a lot of people," says Rikki. "It would have been bad if I'd stayed in school. When there are a lot of people, I feel squished."

The Scandoras are unschoolers, so Rikki has grown up pursuing her deepest interests every day, all day long. "My hobbies are the things I do all the time," she states. "I have flexibility, a schedule that changes depending on how I'm feeling or what the weather is like."

Rikki reads about 20 books every 3 weeks, checked out from her library's naturalist section; she records information from the books in her journals. She rises early, often around 4:30 A.M., and fills early morning hours with journal work and other odds and ends until the rest of the family awakens. She spends some time with them, then takes care of her pet frog, turtle, parrot, mice, fish, two rabbits, and the family dog.

Each day, she walks the mile and a half to a secluded and small wooded area alongside Thornton Creek where listening to birds fills several hours. It's home for lunch and a bit of work on any current projects before heading for a nearby grassy baseball park. There, Rikki spends a couple of hours practicing bagua (a form of martial arts) and a couple more hours doing animal tracking exercises.

"By that time, it's about 5 P.M.," Rikki says, "so I go to a big tree near the park and, at this time of year, watch the sunset for 30 minutes or so. Then I go home, do some craftwork, perhaps work on one of my watercolor paintings of animals, have dinner, journal until 9:30, and go to bed."

Two days a week, Rikki attends the Wilderness Awareness Community School (WACS), carpooling with fellow homeschoolers and sister Rhiannon for the hour-long commute. The two teachers and nine students (between 14 and 19 years old) who make up the class devote one of those days to tracking exercises. Currently, they are following the lives of coyotes who dwell on a nearby sandbar to figure out population, which animals will likely breed, and where they will make their dens.

Rikki is in the third of six levels of the shikari, or tracker, program, having completed, among other things, journals of the tracking of 25 mammals. She's finished the kamana program, an intensive year-long journaling process designed to help a naturalist know the land "as well as a native would have known it." She completed the program so quickly and thoroughly, a teacher from another school has nicknamed her "The Living Legend."

While studying wilderness survival skills, Rikki learned how to skin animals. "I figured stuffing them was pretty much the same thing except for a more careful operation," she says about her growing collection of stuffed birds, which utilizes only roadkill. To find out more about taxidermy techniques, she read some books from the library, but says, "Mostly I've discovered that I improve with practice."

> **The study of survival skills has opened up related avenues of exploration, revealing in an unschooler's life yet again how wide the path of educational freedom can be.**

Shortly after getting involved with WACS, Rikki followed an interest in bagua, and found "a total connection" between the teachings of WACS and her martial arts instruction. "In order to remember 2 hours worth of 'bird talk,' I go into what we call a sense meditation," she explains. "Totally in the now, you can 'listen' with all your senses. Any thoughts you have are going to be distracting. You need to clear your mind."

The study of survival skills has opened up new and related avenues of exploration for Rikki, revealing in an unschooler's life yet again how wide and long the path of educational freedom can be. She is now fascinated by edible and medicinal plants, and the lives of hunter-gatherers, adding more biology, math, and history to a course of study that may seem, to some, at odds with a traditional government school curriculum.

When she turns 18, Rikki plans to attend New Jersey's Wilderness Awareness School, learn as much as she can, perhaps get a job teaching there, and "basically just keep doing what I'm doing right now." She's ruled out becoming a veterinarian or working with the forest service. "They'd have a lot of contact with animals," she says, "but they wouldn't have that hunter-gatherer aspect to it."

She's sure something will open up. "There's increasing interest in scientific research and surveys using trackers and wildlife watchers as opposed to putting radio collars on animals," Rikki says. "I could see doing that."

20

Where in the World?

DAVID BEIHL

Born: June 6, 1985; Colorado Springs, Colorado

Homeschooling: 1990 to present

Family: Parents—Gary and Penny; Siblings—Tommy (12), Debbie (10)

Most memorable wisdom about life or learning: From parents—Pray and study.

Favorite study: Early years—geography, reading; Currently—social studies, math, science, English, still likes to read

Current work: Homeschooling student

Gary and Penny Beihl lived in Texas when their three children were still preschool age. On a whim, homeschooling friends invited them to an upcoming seminar on the topic presented by Dr. Raymond and Dorothy Moore. On the eve of the seminar, baby Debbie got sick, and Gary attended the first day while Penny stayed home.

"He came home and told me, 'Oh, you've *got* to go,'" remembers Penny, who had briefly taught early elementary grades in a small church school. She attended the following day. "I think the Moores convinced my husband about homeschooling somewhat more than me, but I did see some children I thought were homeschooled that seemed like very nice kids. That was impressive. I want my kids to do well academically," Penny adds, "but I want them to be nice people, too." The Beihl family decided to homeschool.

Shortly after the decision was made, the family relocated to rural Saluda, South Carolina, where Gary works for Intel. If he gets home from work in time, he joins Penny, David, Tommy, and Debbie for a 4-mile walk before dinner. Soon after eating, David hits the sack, usually around 8:00 P.M., and then he's off on his morning routine by 6:00 A.M. the next day, running a couple more miles with Dad if time allows before hitting his high-school classes by 8:00 A.M.

"I used to take science, English, American government, and Spanish through videotaped lessons," David explains, "but now I only use the Spanish tape and I never watched the algebra video. My dad is pretty good with math so he helps me with that." Mail-order Bible and typing classes round out the study course for this freshman.

Long before he was a freshman, the seeds for his favorite study, geography, were planted. "*The National Geography Bee* started 11 years ago," David explains. "The first winner was an Adventist, like us, so there was a story about him in the church newsletter. Mom saw this and thought it might be fun for me to do someday. It has a $25,000 scholarship," he adds, "which is a big incentive."

The little boy who started reading when he was 4 years old enjoyed learning the state capitals and studying geography for fun. He did decide to enter the *National Geography* Bee competition, and at 9 years of age tied for third place in the local competition. "I really felt disappointed because I thought I could win, but I didn't really know how hard it was," David says.

In his second try the following year, David won the local competition and went on to place eighth in a state that televises the competition between the top ten contenders. "Having the state bee televised was good preparation for me for the national bee," he explains, "because I learned how to act under the cameras and lights."

In his third attempt, David missed the state's top ten. He was disappointed, but knew he had two more chances before he became too old for the competition. "I studied harder than I had before and we had the advantage of having new study materials that worked well for me." (Author's note: Sorry, gang, Penny is not divulging the name of the materials until her two younger children pass the eighth grade limit on entering the National Geography Bee competition!) This time, David flew through the local and state competitions into the preliminary national competition.

> The little boy who started reading when he was 4 years old enjoyed learning the state capitals and studying geography for fun.

He didn't make the finals at the national level, but "the people who aren't the top ten all sit in the audience and see what happens, even the things that happen off camera so they have a special advantage. A lot of the people who were in the top ten this year were sitting in the audience last year."

David was down to the wire; 1999 was the last year he could participate in the competition. With hard work he made it to the national level, then leapt into the top ten to participate in the final competition. Before the preliminaries, David and his mother prayed for guidance on what to study. "Immediately," says David, "we picked up a map of Central America that showed a small gulf off Honduras, which I learned is the Gulf of Fonseca."

David explains: "You have two chances to miss a question. When you miss two questions, you're out." As the final competition progressed, the field narrowed to David and Jason Borschow of Puerto Rico. The two contestants received the same questions simultaneously. Jason couldn't answer the first question. The answer to the second question involved—you guessed it—the Gulf of Fonseca. Both boys answered correctly. After Jason then missed a question regarding La Niña, David became the 1999 National Geography Bee champ.

As captain of the U.S. team of four, which included the 1998 second-place finisher, homeschooler J. B. Kizer, David participated in the subsequent International Olympiad, a competition reserved for the bee winners of the previous two years. David's team captured the gold medal.

While he's not yet sure where he'll go to college or what he'll study, David plans to put his $25,000 scholarship to good use soon. The family trip to Australia, another of David's bee prizes, should be a memory by the time this book is published.

David credits homeschooling for allowing him the time he needed to succeed in the geography bee. "I think my parents were able to help me study better," he adds, "and to find ways to study that work for me. Even if you have the world's best teachers, they can't work with 20 or 30 children in a way that makes the best use of their different styles of learning; that's just a fact. It works for a lot of kids that can do it, but if you want to really be able to have a special way that works best for you, then homeschooling may be a good option."

21

Sunrise Appreciation 101

LAURA TERIFAY

Born: September 5, 1993; Allentown, Pennsylvania
Homeschooling: 1999 to present
Family: Parents—Paul and Michelle; Siblings—Emily(4), Rebekkah (3), Grace (1)
Favorite study: science experiments and art

Six-year-old Laura has been sledding with her sisters in the newly fallen snow on the family's rural acreage in Pennsylvania. Earlier she helped bake bread, listened to a phonics tape, and practiced counting to 20. Her day sounds like that of countless other young homeschoolers, but Laura has retinitis pigmentosa (RP). Laura is going blind.

One day when Laura was 21 months old, mom Michelle was carrying her toddler across their home's hardwood floor. Laura began screaming, "Stop, there's holes in the floor!" Michelle thought she might be trying to gain attention; baby sister Emily had just been born and kept mom at the hospital for weeks with her own medical problems. When Laura's horror continued, though, Michelle sought a doctor's help.

"I've never heard of such a thing," the doctor told her, and assured a worried mom the behavior would go away. Michelle then enrolled Laura in an Easter Seals program for a few hours each week. "She was late to speak at age 2; that's why she was there," says Michelle. "They didn't know what was causing the strange behavior, either," but they recommended a pediatrician who sent Laura for an eye exam. The initial visit yielded nothing, but the 6-month checkup revealed a change in Laura's retinas. A Philadelphia Children's Hospital specialist made the diagnosis of RP, extremely rare in children that young— Laura was 3 years old by then.

At the supermarket one day about a year later, Michelle was pushing a cart full of groceries through the aisles when 21-month-old Emily, sitting in the cart, began screaming about holes in the floor. "I was heartsick," says Michelle quietly. Emily, too, received the RP diagnosis, as well as one confirming a severe speech disability.

Both little girls have now lost their night and peripheral vision, the two stages that precede loss of central vision and blindness.

Michelle, a teaching degree holder who had grown disgusted with government schools during her student teaching stint, heard about homeschooling before her children were born from lots of friends who were practicing it. "I knew from the first moment I held

Laura that I could never send her off to public school," she says. Later, Michelle also knew that her family couldn't afford to pay out of pocket for the Braille, orientation, and mobility lessons Laura needed. She turned to the local school district for services. Based on the experience of a totally blind student, and without ever having met or evaluated Laura, they insisted that the little girl attend full-day kindergarten. If she didn't, they wouldn't provide services.

"I decided I would probably be down there more often than not arguing with them," Michelle says. "We were arguing back and forth already, and I hadn't even enrolled her." Michelle was horrified when she discovered that the school district used Laura's case as a precedent to deny services to the autistic son of a friend of Michelle's, as well.

A fortunate change in school personnel the following year resulted in a phone call to Michelle from the school, which is now providing the requested services.

A homeschooling day for the Terifays usually includes a doctor's or therapy appointment or two. The girls watch public television's *Bill Nye the Science Guy*, work on a craft project, and play outside. "We usually make bread at least every other day," says Michelle. "The kneading helps Laura's finger strength. We bake and incorporate lessons about fractions into that."

"Right now we're working on a PBS story contest," Michelle continues. "Laura's been writing a page of her story every day and drawing an illustration for it. We go over the Braille cell (to learn how to read letters), and then Laura 'plays' with her Braille writer. She's learning how to make letters. We try to practice numbers every day, usually with the buttons she likes. She counts as high as she can, then she gets to add those buttons to her collection. We just put up a bird feeder, we're planning our garden, and we do a lot of nature walks." Laura asked for rocks and minerals for her last birthday present.

> **The school insisted that the little girl attend full-day kindergarten. If she didn't, they wouldn't provide services.**

Michelle warns me that Laura might not speak on the phone so, just in case, we make alternative plans to fax some questions Michelle can ask her. But Laura has unbundled from winter outerwear and warmed up before taking the phone. "Hello?" The sweetest little voice vibrates my heartstrings.

"I do like to draw," she tells me. "I like to draw puppies best. I like to draw people. I draw pictures of my sisters and hang them on the refrigerator." We talk about buttons and crafts, baking bread, and writing stories. Laura tells me there's nothing that she doesn't like about homeschooling, and concludes by saying that she "teached Becky how to make peanut butter and jelly."

"I think what I'm doing by homeschooling is giving her something she wouldn't get in public school—somebody who loves and cares for her," says Michelle. "A teacher might care, but not the way I do. I can tailor her education to exactly what she needs. In school, she'd be stuck in some special education classroom. That's not what I want for her. Yes, we're getting services from the district, but I don't want her to have labels. I don't want her to feel there's something wrong with her."

At home, Michelle says, "away from judgment and ridicule, she can progress at her own rate, which is really what she needs. I think of myself as a gardener and she's this little precious teeny tiny rose. I'm just giving her the right amount of water and fertilizer so she can unfold into the flower of herself. Gosh, how I treasure each sunrise, sunset, and flower the girls point out to me."

22

At Home and Gifted

GALEN KAUP

Born: July 13, 1983; Potsdam, New York

Homeschooling: 1989 to early college

Family: Parents—David Kaup and Sharon Hotchkiss; Siblings—Melissa (30), Gretchen (23)

Most memorable wisdom about life or learning: From Mom—Your happiness is proportional to your achievements.

Favorite study: Early years—getting started on music; Middle years—getting into "really hard music" and first college course in math; Teen years—college majors in violin performance and math

Current work: Student at Crane School of Music and Clarkson University (Potsdam); co-concert master, Crane Symphony Orchestra

"I'm not sure whose idea it actually was, but I had some input into the matter," says Galen of the Kaup family's decision to homeschool. "I did not enjoy public school. When we finally started homeschooling, I had originally been planning to finish kindergarten, but then I said no, I've had enough of this. I knew why I was being pulled out."

Galen's mom, Sharon, met her husband, David, at work at Clarkson University in Potsdam, New York. She taught biology before coming home; David continues work as a professor there. Still living in the little college town, Sharon shares a glimpse of the family's early homeschooling days.

Little Galen attended Waldorf kindergarten in Minneapolis, Minnesota, for the first semester of kindergarten before the family moved back to New York. It was here that he attended government-school kindergarten. As it had so many times before, the Kaup phone rang one day and the principal was on the other end of the line, nearly in tears.

"Galen has been sent to my office and, while I was dialing your number, he pulled all the books off my shelf and threw them on the floor. Your son has gone unmanageable," the principal told Sharon. "We have no idea what we're going to do with him in first grade."

Sharon replied, "Don't worry about it. We're going to begin homeschooling." She expected, as so many homeschoolers do, to then hear all the reasons why homeschooling is *b-a-d*.

The principal paused, caught his breath, then asked, "You mean—you'd be willing to do that?"

New York State has a propensity for collecting large amounts of paperwork from homeschoolers compared to many other states. "Funny thing is, the school district has never sent me any of the typically required paperwork. I never turned anything in. I think they were scared to call me for fear I'd send the kid back," says Sharon.

Now, one more "problem child" was home to learn. "When I took him out of school, of course, like everybody else, I decided I had to use curriculum. I got the Calvert School second-grade curriculum even though he was coming out of kindergarten. We went through that in 3 months or so. Then I got the fourth grade curriculum and we went through that. Then I bought something else that wasn't really a curriculum, but it demanded a great deal of input from the parent. I liked Calvert because I put it down in front of him and said, 'Here, do good work.'"

"He'd take an hour a day to do two lessons," Sharon continues. "By the time he was 8 years old, or after about 2 years of this, I got tired of saying, 'Put that book away and come do your reading,' and I didn't really do anything more with him. I was running Kumon Math Center (an after-school instruction program that supplements children's school lessons). Galen started doing Kumon math and later Kumon reading, and that's really all the academics he did between the time he was 8 and when he started college at 12."

"I learned how to read when I was two," says Galen, "so I've read practically as long as I can remember. I remember when I got the book *James and the Giant Peach,* I read it through multiple dozens of times. I did the same with Larry Gonick's *Cartoon History of the Universe.* I've got a lot of the Gonick books. I thought this guy was hilarious. I read Calvin and Hobbes books as they came out. I still have some of the newspaper ones, too. I collect newspaper comics as a rather eccentric hobby. I've been collecting them since mid-1990 or so."

> "Galen started doing Kumon math and later Kumon reading, and that's really all the academics he did between age 8 and when he started college at 12."

Violin performances, which began when Galen was 4 years old, have led to two recordings to date, and got him interested enough in getting into Crane School of Music to take the SAT (Scholastic Assessment Test) at age 12. His 1380 score (out of 1600) was enough for acceptance to major in violin performance at Crane when he was 13 years old. At this point,

Galen had already taken four classes over two semesters as a 12-year-old at State University of New York—Potsdam.

If not for homeschooling, declares Galen, "I don't think I'd have been able to accomplish as much. Academically, I would have moved slower. I wouldn't have had as much time, so some of the other things I've done I wouldn't be as good in. Basically, my attributes would be lower generally. Since I wasn't getting along well in school I probably would have become a psychopath or something if I'd stayed for too long. I know I wasn't getting along well with people by the end and I was crazy for a few years afterwards, too. I'm still crazy," Galen laughs, "but not in a psychopathic way like I was."

The non-psychopathically "crazy" teen plans graduate school next, probably for both math and music. "If I find that too much of a pain to bring off," he says, "I could just do one." Galen thinks highly of his hometown, Potsdam, but he is eager to live elsewhere. When he finishes graduate school, his desire to play professionally for a classical orchestra will likely take him to many interesting places.

AUTHOR'S NOTE: While finishing this book, I got to see Galen perform with the Crane School of Music Orchestra during the Goodwill Games opening ceremony in Lake Placid, New York. After a solo as the first chair violin accompanying Bruce Hornsby's performance, Hornsby graciously asked the audience for recognition of the young artist, and then stopped playing the piano to walk into the orchestra and ask Galen for his name. Hornsby returned to his piano, played a few bars of suspense music, and announced, "Galen Kaup." Even though Galen didn't get a chance to say that he's a homeschooler, all folks who sat within 20 rows of me in every direction know so now.

23

Short but Sweet: Homeschooling's Lasting Effect

MOLLY DOMENICO

Born: September 27, 1983; Utica, New York

Homeschooling: 1995–1998

Family: Parents—Orin and Kim; Siblings—Nick (22), Eddie (16)

Favorite study: Sign language classes, history study at home, reading

Current Work: High-school student

The cover of *Teen Voices* magazine proclaimed a homeschooling story, so I picked it up from the "freebie" table at the conference at which I was speaking, and added it to my now bulging pile of "things to read when I get home." I found Molly's short first-person story and wanted to know more.

Molly was perfectly happy in government school's seventh grade when at Christmas break she switched to homeschooling. "It was kind of an experiment," she says of her parents' desire to homeschool with her and her adopted brother, Eddie.

Parents Kim and Orin read a lot about homeschooling and spoke with experienced homeschoolers before taking the plunge. "We weren't sure if it was going to work because we were talking to people who had homeschooled their children from the beginning," Molly explains. "That was different because we'd been to school for so long."

Molly, a self-described "social person and big flirt," missed being around a lot of people, and her friends "were getting boyfriends and none of that happened to me during homeschooling."

Call me old-fashioned, but isn't seventh grade early to begin worrying about boyfriends? "Yeah," Molly admits. "In public schools, people start dating really early. I got a boyfriend the month I went back to school."

> "I just looked around and found out what my interests really were. The kids in public school, all my friends, still don't know what they'd like."

The Domenico family started off with a school-at-home model, but as Kim and Orin kept reading about the practice, they decided a much looser approach was in order, one sometimes called "unschooling." Kim told Molly that since she knew the basics, she didn't have to "keep torturing" herself with math work. "My parents were so into me finding out what I was interested in," says Molly, "that that's what I did. I went to the library all the time and just looked around and found out what my interests really were. The kids in public school, all my friends, still don't know what they'd like. No one ever asks them, so they fill up their spare time with driving lessons, get a car, and work."

Molly discovered a love for sign language. One year, she took the three available classes in sign language at the Board of Cooperative Educational Services (BOCES), a set-up that offers services to groups of small New York school districts, which then share the cost of services utilized. During the following year, Molly completed three more sign language courses at Herkimer College and tucked away the college credits for future use. She even got a chance to share her sign-language talents with a homeschool 4-H group that asked her to teach a class.

Molly also discovered a passion for Egyptology that she plans to pursue once she decides on a college. "I wouldn't have had enough time to myself to discover things I like if it hadn't been for home-schooling. Having time to myself was really important," she says.

Time at home also allowed Molly to earn money "long before I was old enough to get a 'real' job. Word traveled fast in the neighborhood that I was available for baby-sitting," she explains. "It was fun to get to make money while my friends were at school."

Molly feels she had an opportunity "to look at public school from the outside," and found it has a lot of faults. "There are all the kids who don't want to be there," she begins. "You waste so much time in a class you don't like, because you probably won't do anything but memorize something for a test and forget it afterwards. You're not *really* learning."

Mostly, though, Molly recognizes a change in her view of self. "When I went to junior high my whole 'self' was what I look like, how other people see me, and who my friends and I are. I was thinking of who 'we' were and focusing on something that really isn't important—the 'classification'—and judging people by the group they're in. I don't feel that way anymore. I met other homeschoolers and they don't look at you and say, 'This is a grunge person.' They just acted like I was one of them, just another kid."

"It was an awakening for me. It separated me from my friends a bit during that time because I got over what they were into so I wasn't part of it anymore. I had a really hard time communicating with them during that period. I didn't really explain to them why I was homeschooling or what I was learning from it. If I told them anything, it was when I went back to school. I didn't forget anything I learned."

"Junior-high time with its mean atmosphere was a particularly good time to homeschool," Molly notes. "That's why I didn't really have an objection to it, besides that I would miss my friends."

Noting the strength of that social pull once again on a homeschooler clearheaded enough to recognize all the benefits of learning at home, I ask Molly: If a fairy godmother could wave her wand and somehow create a similar social experience outside of government school, would you choose school attendance or homeschooling?

"It would be nice to have that. I would choose outside of school," she says. "I wish the most important part of school was what I'm getting in my classes, but that's not true. I'm not getting what I should be going for."

24

Special (Education) Delivery at Home

CHRIS BUTIKOFER

Born: June 20, 1990; West Minster, British Columbia, Canada
Homeschooling: 1996 to present
Family: Parents—Stefan and Loralea; Sibling: Sophia (7)
Favorite study: Science and art; science experiments are the best
Favorite books: Charlie Brown comics, *Encyclopedia Brown* and *Einstein Anderson* books, *Choose Your Own Adventure* books
Current work: Homeschooling student

Hans Christian Butikofer, better known as Chris, studied math today. He used Professor B Math. "It's real life math, but sometimes it's in books, sometimes on fingers," Chris says from his home in British Columbia. He sounds excited.

Chris's mom, Loralea, chimes in. "It's a special kind of math system that starts a kid again from the bottom up, and it uses the tactile method of fingers. The kids really enjoy it, and I like that it brings theory down to reality again. Chris, even though he's very advanced in math, needs that."

This 9-year-old math whiz wants to be a criminologist someday, because that work includes being both a scientist and a policeman. "And during my spare time, I want to do a few things: baseball and go to space. I play baseball now."

Loralea and Stefan, Chris's dad, just received word that Chris did well on provincial exams, excellent in all areas except for story writing, which was judged acceptable. Canadian law just changed, however, rendering the tests optional for homeschoolers, so they won't be administering them again.

> "We knew there was something wrong from the time Chris was born. He wouldn't conform himself to your body; that's a typical autistic thing to do, but I didn't know that at the time."

If you've read much about homeschooling, you know that the correlation of good test scores and broad interests is not unusual. However, most of the parents of these children don't say, as Loralea does, "We knew there was something wrong from the time Chris was born. He wouldn't conform himself to your body; that's a typical autistic thing to do, but I didn't know that at the time. From about 6 months to a 1 ½ years he was all right. At about 14 months, he got into his terrible 2's and he stayed there until he was 5 years old. It took us having a second child to realize how different Chris was."

At 2½ years old, Chris didn't talk except for a few baby "sound" words. He learned to read before he could speak, a fairly typical progression for autistic children who tend to teach themselves through the whole word method, memorizing the shape of the word. Loralea's parents encouraged her to try phonics, hoping that phonics would help him learn to speak. Loralea's dad, Don Calvert, was working as a homeschooling consultant after retiring from 33 years employment with the Calgary public schools: 7 years as a teacher, 7 as an assistant principal, and 19 as a principal.

"I taught Chris the sounds of letters," says Loralea, "and he caught on quickly because he liked symbols. It took from about the age of 2 into the age of 3 for him to begin to realize that sounds were important. He saw the word 'cat' and made a meow sound. After he began to understand the sound thing, all of a sudden he understood that a cat is 'c-a-t,' you have to say it that way. When he first understood the pronunciation of the word 'cat,' I saw the lights go on for him."

Loralea's parents eventually gifted her and Stefan with the money needed to attend a homeschooling seminar in Alberta. While there, Loralea filled in a little questionnaire on attention deficit disorder (ADD) with information about Chris. On a scale where a child scoring higher than 6 might have ADD, Chris got a whopping 18.

However, Loralea calls Chris's condition "probably undiagnosed autism," and shares her reason for a lack of diagnosis. "I had heard warnings that if you get your child diagnosed, the government is allowed to intervene more easily." The couple decided they'd handled things so far, so a formal diagnosis was unnecessary.

Chris grew to kindergarten age, and "his behavior was abominable. He didn't communicate his feelings. He never got angry; he was either happy or panicking." But Chris continued developing his reading skills, Loralea says, "which made all the difference. Looking back, we see that he may have been called severely autistic. If he hadn't learned to communicate, he would be more severe than he is. The best way for him to learn at that point in his life was jumping up and down on the trampoline while I talked to him."

As Loralea patiently provided necessary attention to her son's special needs, a friend suggested she also try a dose of a grape seed extract, Albinogenol, known to help children like Chris. "Within 20 minutes of taking the first pill, he sat down and colored. He'd never done that before. He was able to concentrate," says Loralea. "Other brands don't seem to work with him," she adds.

When Chris was 6½, Loralea added a dose of folic acid (only fresh). "Within a month, a lot of his weird nervous and Tourette's syndrome type ticks went away," Chris's mom explains. "He stopped biting his nails, flicking his head, scratching, and grunting. He also stopped hitting his friends over the head."

Today, Chris learns with his sister and readily admits that "we get mad at each other and say I'll never play with you again, but then a while after—about 10 minutes—we say, can you play a game with me? We get back together fast, but it doesn't change the fact that we fighted."

Loralea's take on the siblings' relationship is a bit different. "Sophia helped convince Chris that he was a human, not some kind of animal. When she came along, Chris saw she's a human baby who came out of my tummy. He realized, 'I used to be like that.' That had a very humanizing effect on him because before that he was just like a little spinning top."

Recently, Loralea found the Childhood Autism Rating Scale on the Internet (www.paulbunyan.net/users/shannon/cars.htm). She believes that at the age of 2½, Chris rated 47, or severely autistic. Today, she scores him at 27, just within the range of non-autistic. "Cool, huh?" she asks.

Very cool.

25

Business Not Quite as Usual

MAKONNEN DAVID BLAKE HANNAH

Born: February 9, 1985; Kingston, Jamaica

Homeschooling: Birth to present

Family: Parents—Deeb and Barbara

Most memorable wisdom about life or learning: From parents—"Every day is a learning experience and I live life to the fullest. Every piece of advice Mom has ever given me I take into consideration and use in everyday life."

Favorite study: Early years—reading everything; Middle years—reading; *National Geographic* and science-oriented books favorites; Teen years—same; reads everything

Current work: Youth technology consultant for the Jamaican Ministry of Technology and Commerce (since 1998); co-owner Spy-HQ, computer business; music studio engineer; launching a music company

Makonnen David Blake Hannah wakes to the sunshine over Kingston, Jamaica, eats breakfast, and soon gets to work talking on the phone with business partners or providing updates as a consultant to Jamaica's minister of technology and commerce. It's business not quite as usual because Makonnen is a 14-year-old "unschooler," or one who uses the world as his classroom and learns through day-to-day experiences.

Day-to-day experiences have been rich for a young man whose dad runs a music studio and whose mom works as a journalist, author, and film maker. "Many people know me as a Rasta woman who does-n't put her child in school," explains Makonnen's mother, Barbara Blake. "People have recognized him on the street since he was 7 years old and we did our first movie. We didn't think his appointment as government technology and commerce consultant would bring international attention. We just thought, 'Oh, cool, how nice, Phillip. You're a good man to offer this to Makonnen; that's lovely.' But next thing we know the news is all over the world! If he wasn't prepared, it would be crazy, but it's no big thing, just a good thing."

> "We've used a couple of textbooks they use in the schools, but every resource I need is on the Internet, so I just go right there. I'm an Internet-based learner."

Makonnen plans to keep his consulting job as long as the minister wants his help, even though his only monetary compensation has been a small honorarium. "I think you have to be 15 to be paid. I'm not in it for the money, anyway," he explains, "so it doesn't really matter."

What does matter to Makonnen is Internet research for his businesses and consulting job, the Internet lessons he takes, and the books he's currently using to review the computer programming languages Java and C++. "Anything I really have to learn, I usually just sit down and learn it," Makonnen says. "We've used a couple of textbooks they use in the schools, but every resource I need is on the Internet, so I just go right there. I'm an Internet-based learner," he adds with a laugh.

Makonnen's interest in and use of computers began about a decade ago. As a 4-year-old, his writer mom's computer with "the little green blinking screen" fascinated him. "I would sit around and press buttons and I got interested," he says. "As I got older, I got to use newer and newer computers. Now I have a 450 megahertz, 128 meg RAM, a clone I built myself." He credits his growing knowledge to "asking questions of people who know more than I, reading books, and going on the Internet."

Most of Makonnen's business partners are old friends who have already graduated from school, and he has "too many friends" to ever feel socially isolated. "I go out all the time," he says as if the question of social isolation is almost silly. "In Jamaica, we have a lot of opportunity to interact with people because there are concerts and music sessions practically every weekend. I'm always there, so I know everyone. I'm a friendly person, so I have bunches of friends."

When he's not consulting or building or repairing computers, Makonnen works on a Web site he created with two other homeschooling teenagers from the United States (see chapter 17). The site, eBiz 4 Teens (http://library.advanced.org/28188/), "teaches kids how to start up their own Net-based businesses." It was good enough to get the team into the final competition for ThinkQuest, an international cyber competition that this year attracted 3,000 students and coaches from 127 countries. The homeschooling team and their coaches (their moms) flew to Los Angeles for the finals. John Gage, Sun Microsystems creator, presented the homeschooling team with the Interdisciplinary category's Silver Award. Makonnen will forever be the first Jamaican to have participated in the competition.

"It's really all about my thirst for knowledge," says Makonnen about homeschooling. "Whatever I've wanted to do, I've been able to do. Sometimes there might be people who know more about math than I do, but I'm doing things they might not be, so I wouldn't want to compare two different approaches to education."

Makonnen looks forward to his start-up businesses helping his country. "I want to put Jamaica on the map as an information technology power in the Caribbean, to make a little mark on this world," he says. Indeed, his idea of success is "just being happy with whatever you're doing and everyone around you being happy when they are with you. I want to make other people happy the way I make myself happy."

"We're tech activists," says Barbara. "Jamaica's adults know very little or nothing about computers. It has to be the youth that will bring Jamaica into the tech age."

To that end, the Blake Hannah family is working hard, in conjunction with the minister, on setting up a national technology school. "We've opened computer labs at two high schools and intend to do so at every school that wants one. Makonnen's appointment has been a very deliberate act by the minister to draw even more attention to technology in education."

The only other homeschoolers Barbara has met in Jamaica have been Americans or people who have lived abroad. The family is concerned about a national population of which 50 percent are under the age of 25, and an estimated 60 percent exit high school semiliterate with a low level of general knowledge. "It worried me that I was going to have to put my child into this educational system," Barbara explains. "Makonnen learned to read when he was 3 years old. At 5 years of age, I put him into a nice little experimental school with a lovely English woman as a teacher. But everybody else was just learning to read, and I knew he was always going to be ahead of his age group. I was determined not to put my child into the hands of the illiterate barbarians of state schools, so I brought him home. It's been good. It has set a matrix to show

> **"I want to put Jamaica on the map as an information technology power in the Caribbean, to make a little mark on this world."**

other mothers what they can do, and it has shown the educational system what it *should* do. Homeschooling is the best thing that ever happened to us."

This homeschooling mom's own formal education ended with a Kingston, Jamaica, high school diploma, but her education was always supplemented by a "house full of books and magazines and opportunities to meet and talk with intelligent people" who visited her journalist father.

"You know," she concludes, "the Winnie the Pooh books end because Christopher Robin has to go to school at age 6." (The Pooh books were Makonnen's favorites in his early years of reading.) "Up to then, he's been homeschooled. He has to go learn algebra." Jamaica may one day find itself lucky that Makonnen's adventures didn't have to end for compulsory school attendance.

26

Dancing Toward Adulthood

JULIA JAMES

Born: January 3, 1983; Walla Walla, Washington

Homeschooling: Birth to 1995

Family: Parents—Matt and Barbara; Siblings—Jenny (25), Adrian (23), Jocelyn (21), Emma (19), Tom (14)

Most memorable wisdom about life or learning: The best way to learn is when it isn't something an authority figure has planned out for you or told you to do.

Favorite study: Early years—dancing around the house (but not formal classes), music; Middle years—English, writing; Teen years—dance, reading ("I'm in love with Dickens and Jane Austen")

Current work: School of American Ballet (school of the New York City Ballet, since 1997)

Listening to music and performing pirouettes around the house are Julia's earliest memories, long before the goal of becoming a professional dancer loomed possible. "There were, however, things I'd rather have been doing when I was little—like building a tree fort, Julia says. "I didn't start dance classes until I was about 7 years old."

As the fifth of six children, Julia inherited parents who had learned a few things about education as their four oldest children experienced an assortment of schools and educational approaches, including periods of homeschooling, as the family experimented with different lifestyles in Washington, Oregon, and Utah. (Matt's book, *Homeschooling Odyssey,* describes in more detail the often dizzying chronology.)

One by one, all of the siblings joined Jenny, the oldest, in learning at home. Barb notes a transition a number of homeschooling families experience. These families originally remove their children from the government school system as a response to negatives they detect, be they overcrowding, dumbed-down curriculum, questionable socialization, violence, drugs, and/or philosophical differences with the "one right way" attitude towards learning, to name a few. Often the act of homeschooling shifts a family's focus from the initially negative motivation of escaping from the school system to the positive of the obvious benefits that result. "The other children followed into what became such a fun thing to do," says Barb of her family's transition, "that our motivation for homeschooling wasn't any longer a negative thing."

Julia started homeschooling in Utah, where her day began "somewhere around 9 A.M. I usually had to do a lesson in English and in math that I'd get done in the morning. I practiced piano for half an hour each day, then Tom and I usually played outside for a long time until it was time for ballet class."

Julia appreciates that homeschooling provided lots of time to do what she wanted, especially reading and figuring things out for herself. "That's when you really learn, because figuring it out by yourself makes it 'stick,'" she says.

Although happy at home with her family, Julia chose to attend public school in sixth grade, curious about where she stacked up academically. "I discovered I'd been to school for 5 years less than everybody else and I was in the advanced reading group and other things like that. I think it's because I went into it fresh. Everybody else was sick of school by that point."

"By eighth grade, I was ready to go back home," says Julia, "so I started the concurrent program at the University of Utah, where I took university ballet classes as a high-school student. In ninth grade, I only went to school until lunch."

Julia carried her extra energy to dance classes, too. "I was able to go to ballet and just give myself up to it and not have to worry about what else was going on. I wasn't worn down with other things. My teacher always asked me what vitamins I took because I was the bounciest one in the class. I think that had a lot to do with homeschooling. I don't know if I would still be dancing if it wasn't for homeschooling."

But Julia *is* still dancing, invited at age 15 to attend via scholarship the prestigious School of American Ballet in New York City. "At first I was intimidated by the reputation of the company," Julia explains, "and I'd heard everything about New York City, too. But I'd been at the school for 5 weeks in the summer, so I kind of knew what I was getting into."

Julia also attends Professional Children's School between ballet classes. "It's like a high school except there are only about seven people in each class," she says. "There aren't any electives, just the basics. Each day I walk to school—rain or shine—and attend four classes for 45 minutes each."

> But Julia *is* still dancing, invited at age 15 to attend via scholarship the prestigious School of American Ballet in New York City.

Opportunities for art and culture abound now that Julia lives and works near Lincoln Center. "We get to go to New York City Ballet performances for free because we go to their school," reports an excited Julia. "We get discounted student tickets for other things; we can sit in the nosebleed section of the Metropolitan Opera for just $25!"

Now 17, Julia plans to go to college, possibly to study in the environmental field so she can combine her interests in journalism, photography, and the outdoors. She'd like to defer entry, though, to work with a professional dance company first. Her future might also hold continued travel and, eventually, a large family. "I don't want to send my children to public school. I think homeschooling makes your family so much stronger and sets you apart from other kids. Even if they're getting the same education as you are, homeschooling gives you something that makes you feel different from other people. It's fun to have that experience that not everybody has."

> **"I don't want to send my children to public school. I think homeschooling makes your family so much stronger and sets you apart from other kids."**

Today, only the youngest James child, Tom, still lives at home. "It's a weird feeling when you have six kids and you drop down to that last one," says Barb. The joy of homeschooling remains, however.

"The days I remember being so wonderful were when we could look out our window and down the little hill and see the public school," says Barb. "I'm sure the kids were having a nice day, but when the snow was falling and we were cuddled up on our sofa reading *Treasure Island,* moving on to making gingerbread men, and playing the music we wanted to be listening to, I mean, how much more wonderful can it get than that?"

27

Around the States in 50 Weeks

AMY BURRITT

Born: January 19, 1983; Traverse City, Michigan
Homeschooling: 1989 to present
Family: Parents—Kurt and Emily; Sibling—Jon (11)
Most memorable wisdom about life or learning: From parents—
Once you start a project, don't quit halfway through.
Favorite study: English literature, reading, writing
Current work: Coffee shop waitress

On what *seemed* just a typical night after dinner, Kurt and Emily Burritt sat their homeschooling children down and asked them, "What would you think about going on a trip across the country, visiting all 50 states in 50 weeks—and maybe meeting their governors?"

The question was a surprise to 12-year-old Amy, whose mind immediately filled with more questions: "What about my friends? The dog? Our house?"

Many homeschooling families have discovered the educational benefits of travel, and take or make opportunities to incorporate it into their lifestyle. Amy didn't know that her parents had been figuring out how to make this trip work for several years before they popped the question to their children. "Kurt and I wanted to show the kids what the country was all about," says Emily, "and spend some quality time together as a family. When they got to the ages where we knew they would really remember it, absorb it, and it would be good for them," she continues, "we sold our business, rented out our house, and took off in a motor home." The goal to meet all the governors along the way served to focus the trip on learning about politics and government, as well as to keep Amy from missing her friends so much "that I'd want to come home and give up the whole thing."

> The goal to meet all the governors focused the trip on learning about politics and government, and kept Amy from missing her friends so much.

The trip was named "America Through the Eyes of a Student," a slogan proudly printed on sweatshirts, 2 of which were eventually signed by all 50 governors—just barely. When the Burritts arrived at the California capitol, then Governor Pete Wilson was preparing to fly to a business meeting. "His secretary grabbed our sweatshirts, jumped into her car, drove to the airport, and got him to sign the sweatshirts just as he was boarding the plane," remembers Amy. "This trip was a team effort between all 50 governors and my family."

Amy's role on this team was twofold. "From the day we made that decision," she says, "I began practicing interviewing and perfecting my public speaking, as Mom and Dad gave answers they thought the governors might give."

"While practicing to interview Maryland's Governor Parris N. Glendening, I asked Dad, 'What did you want to be when you grew up when you were a kid? What were your goals?'"

Kurt answered, "Well, I always wanted to be a fireman."

"C'mon, Dad," Amy responded, a bit annoyed. "They're not going to say that; be realistic."

When the interview appointment arrived, Amy asked Governor Glendening the same questions. "I think when I was young," said the governor, "I always wanted to be a fireman."

Father and daughter exchanged smiles, and Amy realized Dad had been "right on target."

Amy was indeed the interviewer, the gatherer of information. But she was also the chronicler, faithfully recording daily events in a journal each night.

At one point in the trip, Amy was ready to give up. She was tired of living in a motor home, bored with interviewing governors, and wanted to be "just a normal kid."

Emily and Amy talked—and talked—and Emily presented her daughter the option to quit. Lights came on for Amy. "I realized that if I did go home, I'd have to tell my friends and family that I'd given up. The media had followed the story—some of the television stations had been documenting it—and I'd have to tell them that I quit, and face failure. I wasn't prepared to do that. That's when it became *my* project. That's when things turned around for me; I saw real purpose behind it."

> Amy began crunching her journal into her computer in book format, spurred by Kurt's promise: "You write a book, we'll make sure it gets published, even if we do it ourselves."

Upon returning home, Amy began crunching her journal into her computer in book format, spurred by Kurt's promise: "You write a book, we'll make sure it gets published, even if we do it ourselves."

Amy, Emily, and a writer friend went to work for a year and, in May 1998, the Burritt family produced *My American Adventure.* Home state Michigan Governor Engler joined in celebrating the premiere party for the book. Local news coverage became a widely distributed Associated Press story that captured the attention of television producers for the likes of the *NBC Today Show* and *CBS This Morning.* The Burritts realized their print run of 3,000 copies was no longer enough. They hurriedly enlisted the aid of a literary agent who handled media contacts and sold republishing rights to HarperCollins Zondervan. The publishers were so impressed with *My American Adventure* that they offered Amy a six-figure advance. Zondervan also snatched up rights to the accompanying book, *My Extreme Dream Journal,* which "is where other people can write down their dreams and goals and work on accomplishing them," says Amy.

While not studying or working as a waitress, which Amy enjoys because "a lot of new people come in and I get to meet them," she sings, write songs, and plays a lot of guitar music. "I write and play a folky style of music. A lot of people tell me I sound like Joan Baez."

Now "a high school senior" at 16 and awaiting her SAT (Scholastic Assessment Test) scores, Amy is exploring college options with an eye toward communications and/or journalism.

"It's hard to put into words the way homeschooling has shaped me," says Amy. "Homeschooling provided the opportunity to do these things. Being able to spend the time with my mom, dad, and Jon has been great."

28

Project 2000: Ideals in Motion

TAJ SCHOTTLAND

Born: June 5, 1989; Brattleboro, Vermont
Homeschooling: Birth to present
Family: Parents—Jon and Julie; Siblings—Jared (deceased), Ruby (2)
Most memorable wisdom about life or learning: From parents—
It's fun to learn, you don't have to learn one thing, and you can learn
anything you want.
Favorite study: Woodworking and piano

After reading *The Hobbit,* a book declared his new favorite, Taj is now deep into *King Arthur,* the 10-year-old explains from his home in the Brattleboro, Vermont, countryside. An early reader, Taj also emerged as an early public speaker, tagging along at the age of 6 when his father, Jon, visited schools to talk about his nonprofit organization, Seeds of Peace (dedicated to advocating and teaching ways to practice peace in all aspects of life). "I had a hunch he was going to have an effect," Jon remembers. "What I could tell the children as an adult wasn't nearly as effective as the peer role model Taj is."

One need only speak briefly with Taj to realize the sensitivity of the active young boy who enjoys basketball, baseball, and soccer. After many school visits with Dad, Taj consulted with his mother to create Project 2000.

"Kids were totally mean in school," he explains. "They were punching each other, and everyone would race and hit to be first in line. I thought since the year 2000 was coming up, I would encourage people to do 2,000 good deeds before then. At first, I wasn't sure because I thought it would be a lot of work, but I decided to try it. Once I started, I couldn't stop because it was the right thing—even when it was hard."

With the help of fellow homeschoolers Leigh and Samantha Elliott, as well as his parents, Taj spread the word. The team created a newsletter and a brochure, and Jon designed a Web site. "I would write down what needed to be updated on the page, and Dad would put it up," says Taj.

A friend of Jon's, a reporter for the *Rutland Herald,* wrote a story about Project 2000. The *Brattleboro Reformer* followed suit, and there were more school presentations, including one to an assembly of 300 children. All of this led to 43 individuals and schools pledging to complete their 2,000 good deeds. "I have no idea exactly how many people that is," Taj says, "because the school sign-ups include a lot of people."

Taj believes homeschooling plays a major role in Project 2000. "If I wasn't a homeschooler," he explains, "I wouldn't have time to run the project because I'd be in school all the time. Plus this helps my homeschooling. Now I know how to write paragraphs and letters, and what the purpose of a newsletter is. I know how to get people more involved."

Project 2000 isn't a daily, or even weekly routine. "Sometimes I work intensely on it, and sometimes I let weeks pass and not work on it." It's a loose schedule that fits perfectly into the Schottland family's lifestyle of activity that changes with the weather, though most days for Taj include play with baby sister Ruby, sports, and reading." Notebooks in which Taj can write about the things he learns serve in place of textbooks.

> Taj believes homeschooling plays a major role in Project 2000. "If I wasn't a homeschooler," he explains, "I wouldn't have time to run the project."

Winter is a good time for projects like constructing a papier-mâché solar system. In the summer, "We go swimming and boating in our pond, and we fill out a survey for the Vermont Public Interest Research Group on frog deformities we find. I help run the greenhouse before we get everything planted," Taj adds. "I mix the soil, and plant and water the seeds. I help Dad with the vegetables and Mom with the flowers."

Taj's own Project 2000 good deeds include doing the dishes without being told, stopping his cat from going outdoors to catch mice, changing the cat's litter, training the dogs, and, most frequently, playing with kids at the schools he visits. "Normally, all the kids want to play with me, and then there are one or two kids that no one respects. So I'll probably go over to them, perk them up, and help them."

It's late October 1999 when I ask Taj how close to 2,000 good deeds he is. "Oh, I'm past 2,000," he replies. "I think I'm around 2,300."

At this point, I'm imagining a world well populated with Taj's and blurt out, "How do you think you got to be this way?"

"Well," he says, "Mom and Dad are great. And—I think this is part of it—I had another brother, Jared, who died when he was 12 and I was almost 5. He was really caring to all the creatures. I think I learned a lot from him."

I ask Jon about the brothers' ability to spend their brief time together. "Jared had cerebral palsy and a brain injury at birth. He was profoundly physically disabled, he didn't grow or develop, and eventually his body just gave out," says Jon. "Taj spent all his time with him. Jared couldn't walk, so instead of sitting painfully in a chair, he would crawl and creep a bit. Taj was on the floor with him, so they grew up right next to each other."

The family's learning lifestyle included lots of read-aloud time, "and we tried many reading programs with Jared. Taj was right there, listening, learning, and pointing to the words we always had on cards around the house. Jared's greater communication was limited to raising his arm to say yes, or shaking his head to say no. But Taj was with him always, and learned deeper communication when he was just 2 or 3 years old. I think it was a gift to Taj to have someone so different be his brother, and have it be so normal to him. I think it gave Taj an incredible sensitivity."

At age 10, Taj admits he hasn't given much thought to the definition of a successful life yet but, he says, "I'd like to go out to schools like my dad because sometimes I just feel so sad for the kids. Some of them are alone or teased or not in the 'in crowd.' I want to help them when I'm older."

Taj wants other children to know that homeschooling is "fun, and you can be with kids just as much as if you were in school. There are a lot of homeschoolers out there."

Afterword

Chuck Dobson is not Jedediah Purdy. Aaron Fessler is not Elan Rivera. Monique Harris is not Edward Rembert . . . well, you get the idea.

Isn't that wonderful? Isn't that the commonality and the beauty of their lives, of the lessons they've taken into adulthood, of their definitions of success? Maybe *individuality* is what comes from spending some time growing in freedom, liberated from compulsory attendance at school.

Quite a few of our homeschoolers tend toward self-employment, working in a family business, or freelancing. Does this make for good cogs necessary to the machinery of our economy? Not really. It more likely will create families who become masters of their own economic reality, free of the whims of corporate America. Maybe an *independent spirit* is what comes from spending some time growing in freedom, liberated from compulsory attendance at school.

Did you notice how many began work early—as employees, volunteers, teen entrepreneurs, or workers in a parent's business? This gave them an education in the conduct of business, and at the same time as it allowed them to socialize with a broad range of individuals most often older than themselves. Working from a young age meshed well with a great sense of responsibility for their own education while at home. Maybe *self-reliance* is what comes from spending some time growing in freedom, liberated from compulsory attendance at school.

Many of these folks—whatever their current age might be—state that they don't know what the future holds, in large part because they see so many options available. They are, by and large, happy in their work. Many are pursuing interests that emerged when they were children, took root as they grew, and, because of homeschooling, became early proficiencies. They are doing what they love, and the money is following—to varying degrees, but always enough for them to continue pursuing goals and dreams. Maybe *vocational happiness is* what comes from spending some time growing in freedom, liberated from compulsory attendance at school.

I do not mean to imply that traditionally schooled folks aren't similarly individualistic, independent, self-reliant, and happy in their work; of course, many are. What I'm marveling at—yet again, because I've heard similar anecdotal evidence so many times before—is the seemingly high percentage of these qualities among the homeschoolers in this book. I chose this group of individuals not by those traits but because their lives display many different homeschooling approaches in a variety of geographic settings with varying amounts of parental involvement for different lengths of time and for different reasons. Knowing how worried so many parents are when new to homeschooling (as I was, too) might I now be so bold as to suggest that it would be a lot harder to mess up homeschooling than it is to succeed with it?

As long as we breathe, life is a work in progress. I can't foresee where any of the people we've just met will be in 10, 25, 40 years, but I'd be willing to bet that no matter what life's external forces may shower upon them, in their hearts they will remain relatively happy people, people we would be glad to call our neighbors, friends, family, or church mates.

We as a society make compulsory school attendance and graduation the goal for so many of our children. It has become such a time-consuming goal that our children's personal interests—those interests infused with passion—take a back seat or, worse, wither away, unnurtured and unattended.

Life without the constraints of compulsory attendance means more time to attend to those personal interests. Often, it means the crucial time needed to know one's self well enough to discover what those personal interests are in the first place. Only by removing the externally imposed, consuming goal of compulsory school attendance will even more children enjoy the time and the room in life necessary for personal interests to become known. What a wonderful world it would be.

INDEX